One Girl's Story

By Cecily Gray

Copyright © 2020 Cecily Gray

First published 2020

Disruptive Publishing

17 Spencer Avenue

Deception Bay QLD 4508

Australia

WEB: www.disruptivepublishing.com.au

Book Cover by Cecily Gray

All rights reserved. No part of this publication may be reproduced, stored in or introduced in to a database and retrieval system, or transmitted in any form or by any means (electronic, mechanical, photocopying, recording or otherwise) without the prior written permission of both the owner of the copyright and the above publishers.

ISBN# 978-0-6486989-8-2

The floral emblems on the front cover represent the

Countries of my ancestry

- Scotland – Thistle
- England – Rose
- Ireland – Shamrock
- Australia. – Golden Wattle
- Guugu Yimithirr - Cooktown Orchid

Table of Contents

Chapter One 1
  Introduction 1
Chapter Two 3
  Yarrabah 3
Chapter 3 8
  Aboriginals Protection and Restriction of the Sale of Opium Act of 1897 8
Chapter 4 10
  The Grandparents 10
Chapter 5 14
  The Grandparents 14
Chapter 6 17
  Tibby McAndrew 17
Chapter 7 27
  Samuel Myquick 27
Chapter 8 32
  Hull River Settlement 32
Chapter 9 38
  The Cyclone 38
Chapter 10 43
  Dunk Island 43
Chapter 11 46
  Palm Island 46
Chapter 12 60
  Mapoon Mission 60
Chapter 13 64
  Cooktown 64
Chapter 14 68
  The Gortons 68
Chapter 15 76
  An Exemption 76
Conclusion 78
Appendix: The Aboriginal Protection And Restriction Act 79

Chapter One
Introduction

This is the story of an Australian child who was born in captivity. Her name is Gladys and she was my mother.

I now put my pen to paper to tell the story of her once mysterious childhood. It is a story that needs to be told and unless I do, I fear it will be lost forever, taken to the grave with me. My wish is that my children and my children's children, will know her story and understand a little of the legacy they have inherited.

I saw my mother to be strikingly attractive in her appearance, slim, well-spoken, intelligent, and knowledgeable. Her manner gave no indication other than that she had been raised as a 'European' Australian. She made the most of her limited resources and always dressed smartly, taking good care of her health and that of her family. She worked hard and strove to give us the best she could.

Throughout my childhood I was curious about her background. She was very taciturn about this. I would ask questions but most often only brief, throwaway answers were given. However, there were moments when she would wax lyrical about her life in North Queensland.

Her tales involved riding giant sea turtles down to the water, seeing mother dugongs weeping for their captured babies and pearl divers collecting trochus shells, travelling on steamships, being lifted up onto a roof by Rev John Flynn to retrieve a shot chicken hawk and many more such adventures.

Very occasionally she would let something slip. Like, her mother had pale skin and blue eyes. And one that came completely out of the blue – her sisters rode horses. Who and where were these sisters? I had wrongly assumed that she had no family and had been brought up in an orphanage. I thought the only reason she didn't tell us about them was that she didn't know herself!

These clues plus her physical appearance, gave me to suspect that she had a rather exotic heritage. Once when I was about ten years old, I was brushing her long, dark silky hair, and I asked her if she was an "Islander". She replied quite dismissively, "Oh, something like that". And that was the end of the matter.

But over the years various members of the family were given titbits of information by way of little stories she would tell. As adults, we were astounded when by chance, we discovered that she had visited Victoria in her youth. That was no mean feat as the journey from North Queensland in those days would have meant days, perhaps weeks, by boat. She had seen the fairy penguins at Phillip Island and the Twelve Apostles. The Great Ocean Road would have been quite newly opened at the time. She talked about Dr Banfield and his reclusive life on Dunk Island and many other aspects of Northern Queensland life between the two world wars.

As the years passed, I was always troubled by the fact that I knew so little about my mother prior to the late 1930s. I felt concerned that she seemed to have no extended family of her own and so after I retired in 2001, I began to think seriously about investigating this. It was the fact that she would often let down her guard to me and other family members that caused me to feel in my heart, that she really was tired of all the secrecy. Regardless, I knew I couldn't rely on her cooperation with this.

I had suspected she had been reared on a mission so I thought gaining information about them would be a good place to start. In 2006 I found this pamphlet:

"Community and Personal Histories"

Armed with this my journey began. There were lots of hits and misses but this gave me contacts mainly by way of the internet to:

- the *Queensland State Archives*,
- the *Anglican Church Archives*,
- the *John Oxley Library*, and
- The *Yarrabah Mission Museum*.
- I personally visited the Search Room at the State Archives at Runcorn Brisbane.
- At the *Aboriginal and Torres Strait Islander Multicultural Affairs Department in William* St Brisbane, my request for a search was instigated. (No. 2009/0286).
- I sincerely thank *Kathy Frankland* for her interest and assistance and
- *Andrew Walker* for the time and effort involved in his comprehensive report which he presented to me in September 2012.
- Thanks also to Marge Scully *Cooktown Historical Society*

Chapter Two

Yarrabah

My first discovery in 2009, was in the Yarrabah Mission's Baptism Records which had been uploaded to the internet. I had never heard of Yarrabah but through determination and divine intervention (something I have sensed throughout this experience), there it was! After scrolling through hundreds of entries, I found with great exultation, my mother's and her mother's (Tibby Mc Andrews), names registered there. So now I finally had something solid with which to begin.

Although I already had this in hard copy in 2009, it wasn't until 2011 when I visited Yarrabah that I was able to view the original documents. I was kindly given permission to photograph the original old book. It was quite intact although showing the deterioration of its hundred or more years.

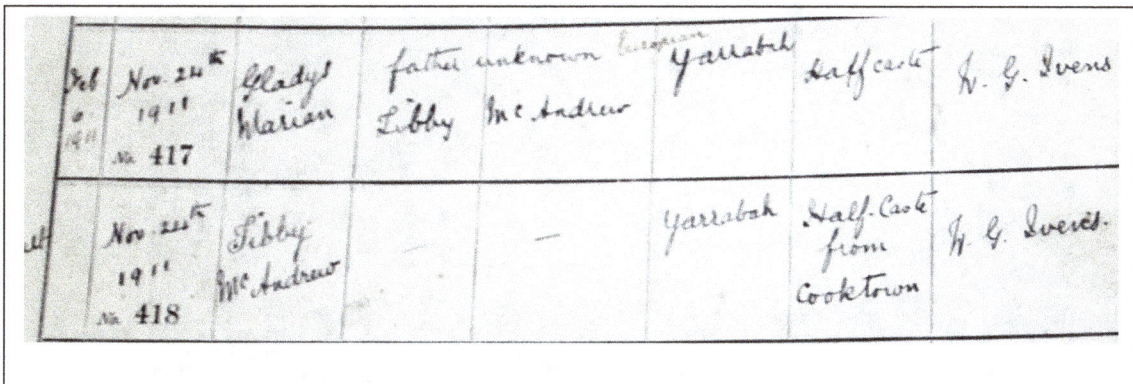

Yarrabah Baptism Register

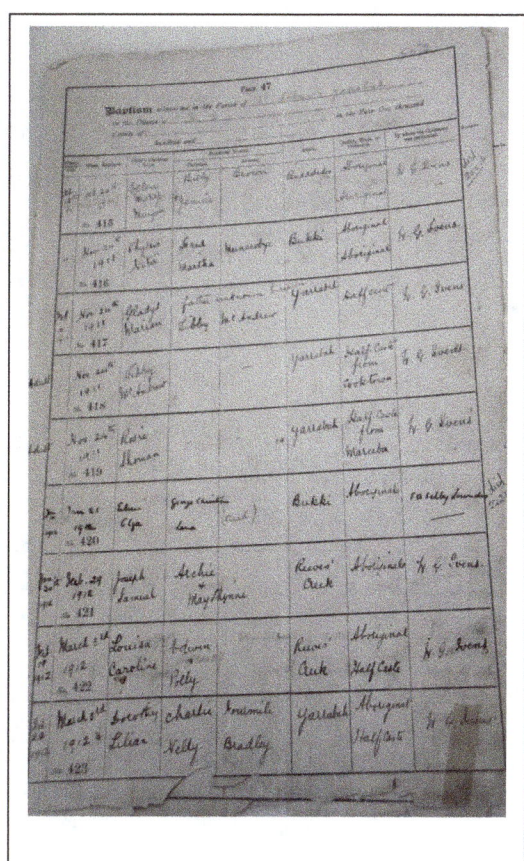

The records show that Tibby and Gladys were both baptised in St Albans Anglican Church Yarrabah in November 1911. Gladys's birthdate is recorded as 6th February 1911. Tibby's father is registered as Robert McAndrew and her mother, just Maggie. Gladys's father is recorded as Unknown European. Of course, no paternal grandparents were registered.

St Albans Church Yarrabah 1909 *(Photographs from John Oxley Library)*

Albans Church Yarrabah 2011

Plaque on St Alban's Church

The "Dada" Gribble whose name is on the plaque has a fascinating story of his own.

Ernest Gribble became the Anglican Missionary Priest at Yarrabah in 1904, taking over from his father who had founded the mission in 1893. He oversaw a regimental style of operation of the mission.
He voluntarily retired from his position at Yarrabah under controversy in 1910.

He was later appointed to the Forrest River Mission in Western Australia. Where he was hailed for exposing the large-scale massacre of aborigines in 1926.
He was chaplain at Palm Island Settlement 1929-1931.

Ernest Gribble

Mission at Yarrabah late 19th century or early 20th century: *(Photograph obtained from Yarrabah Mission Museum)*

The birth register records my mother as Gladys Marian. Although we knew her only as Gladys Sylvia, she had told us that she was once named Marian. So this discrepancy cast no doubt for me, that this record was hers. She had also said that her mother's name was something like 'Tabatha'. So once again, 'Tibby' McAndrew was feasible.

Each of the names on this record i.e. Tibby, Robert Mc Andrew, Maggie and 'Unknown European' will be dealt with as I progress chronologically. As too, others who may crop up.

My mother's name being placed in the Yarrabah Baptism Register is a direct result of the passing of The _Aboriginal Protection and Restriction of the Sale of Opium_ Act in 1897, - years before she was even born.

The altruistic purpose of this Act was to "Protect" half-caste aboriginal people from exploitation by the white community (refer Appendix 1). Unfortunately, to implement this it was deemed necessary to ostracise these people and incarcerate them onto purposely built government settlements or church-run missions. It is difficult to understand how this incarceration would help Tibby when the "bird had already flown". But there she was, cast out from her home in Cooktown and transported all the way to Yarrabah near Cairns. Was this really for her benefit or was it to save a scandal for those she had come to love and trust? What was the outcome for the father of the child? Was he imprisoned too, or did he go on to enjoy his privileges in white society?

Yarrabah Mission late 19th early 20th centuries: _(Photograph from Yarrabah Mission Museum)_

Chapter 3

Aboriginals Protection and Restriction of the Sale of Opium Act of 1897[1]
(Refer also to Appendix 1)

By the late 19th century, many in Queensland believed that the Aboriginal people, greatly reduced in number because of dispersal, malnutrition, opium and diseases, were a "dying race". The Queensland Government, under pressure from sections of the community, commissioned Archibald Meston to assess the issue. Meston made a number of recommendations, some of which underpinned the *Aboriginals Protection and Restriction of the Sale of Opium* Act of 1897. [2] Though the Act's creators considered it a solution to a short-term problem, its administrators used it as a device for social engineering and control. Public servants rather than politicians oversaw much of the decision-making, and individual protectors had substantial autonomy in how they implemented the Act.

The Act could be used to justify definitions of Aboriginality bandied about at the time, but even with the help of the Act, they were often contradictory and generally subject to interpretation or variation. For example, in 1905, Queensland's Chief Protector of Aboriginals cited the Act to define a "half-caste" as "any person being the offspring of an aboriginal mother and any other than an aboriginal father – whether male or female, whose age, in the opinion of the Protector does not exceed sixteen, is deemed to be "half-caste". The Chief Protector then went on to describe a "quadroon" as the "offspring" of a half-caste woman by a "white, etc." (Presumably other non-Aboriginal) father.

It was the first instrument of separate legal control over Aboriginal people, and, according to historian Henry Reynolds, it "was far more restrictive than any (contemporary) legislation operating in either New South Wales or Victoria and implemented a system of tight controls and closed reserves.

Archibald Meston

!852-1924

Southern Protector of Aboriginals

For Queensland 1898-1903

---

[1] *Wikipedia 19/6/20*
[2] *Documenting a Democracy, Museum of Australian Democracy. Retrieved 8 February 2020*

The Bureaucrats

The following passage gives a little of the background to the officials whose names will appear on documents concerning Tibby McAndrew's welfare.

Walter E Roth (1861 – 1933) was the first appointed Northern Protector of Aboriginals and was based in Cooktown.

From 1904 -1906 he was Chief Protector Qld and part duty was to record Aboriginal culture.

The first of three bulletins on North Qld ethnology were published in 1901.[3]

He travelled extensively across North Queensland acquainting himself with the local cultures and languages.

In his role as Protector, Roth was responsible for the" removal " of half-caste children to church-run missions away from the influence of tribal customs and white exploitation.

Walter Roth

James King became Northern Protector of Aboriginals on Roth's promotion to Chief Protector Queensland in 1904.

Although a European, **John Kenny** was a constable with Cooktown Native Police. This was not unusual. He later retired from this position and was to eventually become superintendent at the Hull River Mission.

"Ex-Constable John Kenny died in1918 during a cyclone at the Hull River Aboriginal Mission where he was superintendent.[4]

In 1899 Kenny had survived another cyclone (Mahini –the deadliest recorded in Australian history) while in pursuit of miscreants in Princess Charlotte Bay Cape York.

---

[3] *The Roth Family Anthology, A Colonial Administrator (2008)*
[4] *" The Secret War: A True History of Queensland's Native Police Force: European service in the Native Police Force by Jonathan Richards*

Chapter 4
The Grandparents
Maggie

It is unfortunate that I have been unable to uncover a great deal about Tibby's mother (my great-grandmother) Maggie. It is recorded that as a child, Tibby lived with her mother on the cattle station 'Sonata' near Cooktown. Maggie was employed by the owners.

During my communications with relatives now living on Palm Island, I was able to find that she belonged to the Guugu Yimithirr people of the Cooktown area.

The **Guugu Yimithirr** are an Australian Aboriginal tribe of Far North Queensland many of whom today live at Hopevale, which is the administrative centre of Hopevale Shire. At the 2011 census, Hopevale had a population of 1,005 people. It is about 46km from Cooktown by road. It is also the name of their language. They were both a coastal and inland people, the former clans referring to themselves as "saltwater people"

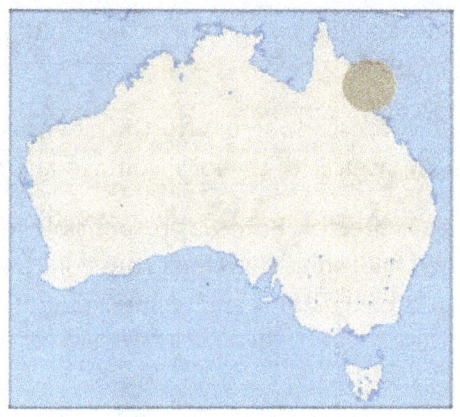

Location of the Guugu Yimithirr people

"In mid-1770, James Cook spent seven weeks ashore at what is now called Cooktown, in north-east Queensland, while his craft, HMS Endeavour, was repaired from damage sustained on the Great Barrier Reef. His interaction with the local Guugu Yimidhirr nation was generally cordial and showed a quite different attitude from that of Dampier. If there is no language in common, one can still exchange names. Cook's crew presumably offered their names and the locals responded. They were introduced by name, 'a ceremony which, upon such occasions, was never omitted'. The Guugu Yimidhirr often came on board ship: 'We had another visit from four of the natives. Three of them had been with us before, but the fourth was a stranger whose name, as we learnt from his companions who introduced him, was Yaparico'." [6]

It is quite feasible that Maggie was related to Yaparico..

The word 'kangaroo' was given to the world by the Guugu Yimithirr people but was mispronounced from 'gangurru'.

Walter Roth worked among the Guugu Yimithirr people both in his capacity as Chief Protector of Aboriginals and as an official recorder of his observations of their culture. By 1899 He was well

---

[5] *https://en.wikipedia.org/wiki/Guguu_Yimithirr*

[6] *R M W Dixon, 'Australia's Original Languages – An Introduction'' Pp 37*

acquainted with the German Missionaries, Messer's Schwarz and Poland at the **Cape Bedford Mission** which he had visited several times.

"On the 8 and 9 March 1899 the mission was damaged by the massive cyclone which also destroyed North Queensland's pearling fleet. Several buildings were unroofed and the mission boat damaged, and again Schwarz, with a keen eye on public effects, got one of the mission girls, Magdalen Mulun, to write to Parry-Okeden to request a new boat"[7]

In Roth's 1901 Report to the Home Secretary's Department, he includes Magdalen's letter.

- *"The letter is remarkable in that it is possibly the first text in an aboriginal language in Queensland, In 1898 Roth was appointed as the first northern protector of Aboriginals under W. E. Parry-Okeden, Based at Cooktown, his main brief was to prevent the exploitation of Aborigines, particularly in employment and marriage. He was also responsible for the regulation of Aboriginal and Torres Strait Islander employment in the beche-de-mer industry. Roth had a scientific background and had trained as physician and anthropologist and published numerous articles on the Aboriginal people of North Queensland. Many of these were compiled into his publication <u>Ethnological studies among the north-west-central Queensland Aborigines</u>; others were submitted for journal articles for publication by organisations such as Royal Society of Queensland."*

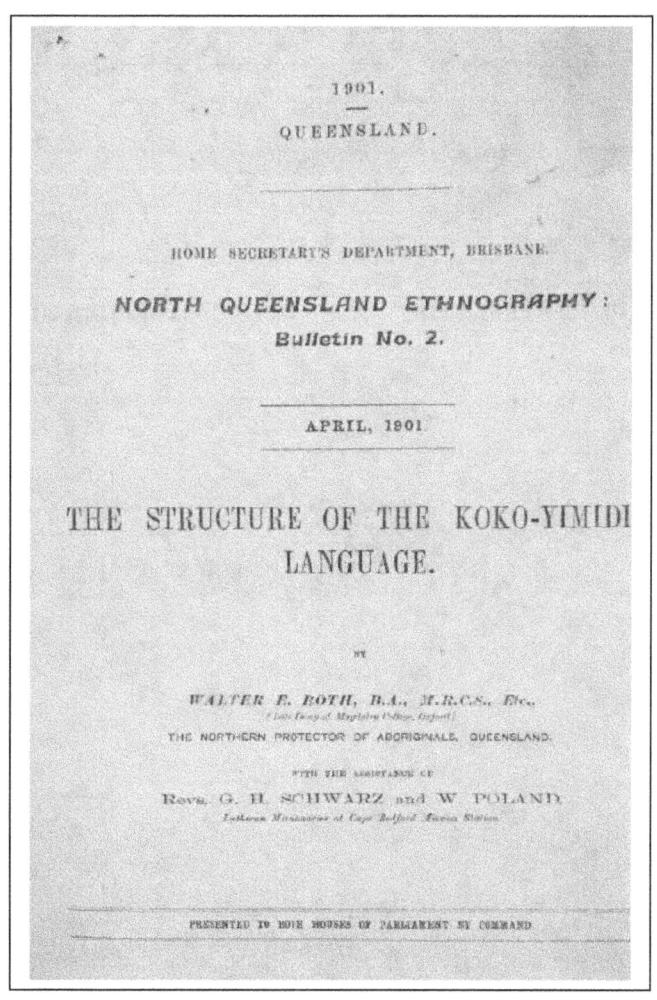

---

[7] <u>Flierl, Johann "My Life and God's Mission, an autobiography by Senior Johann Flier, Pioneer Missionary and field inspector in New Guinea, Lutheran Church of Australia 1899 P164</u>

"Koko-Yimidir" is what Roth called "Guugu-Yimithirr".

Below is a copy of the original letter held by the **Queensland State Archives Series 7328 Item 271655** which was sent to the Commissioner of Police from Magdalen Mulun (of Cape Bedford Mission) via Dr Roth, Cooktown 23 March 1899 (5031/1899).

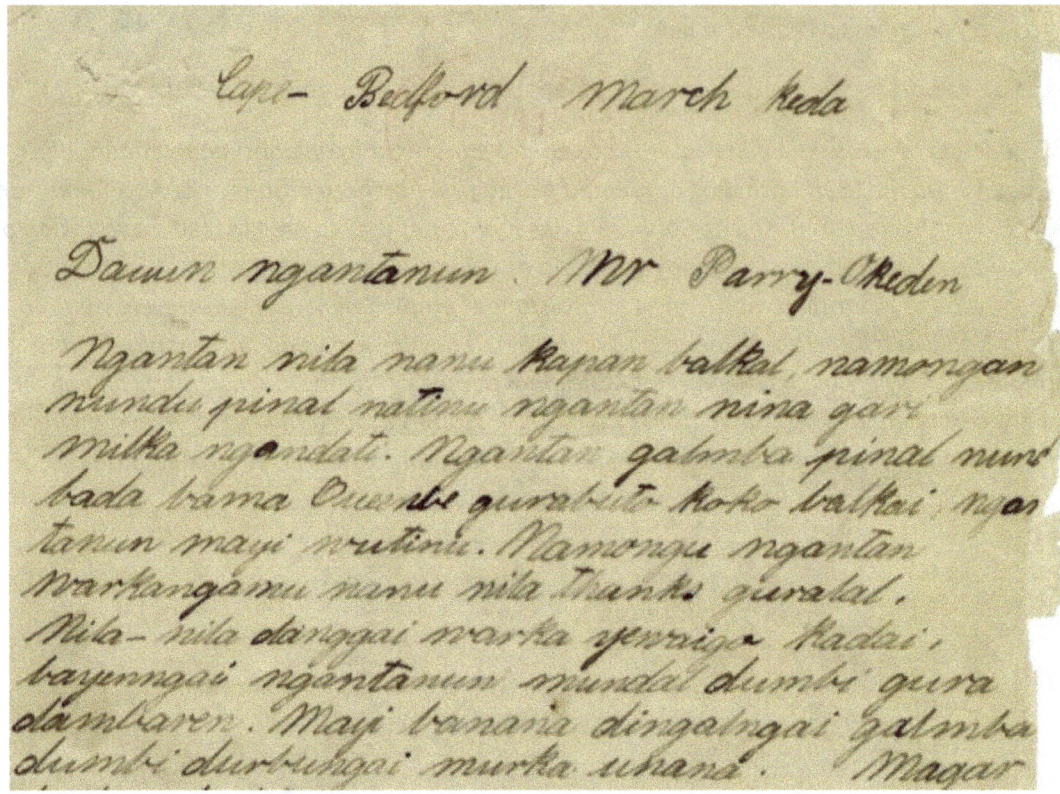

Roth forwards the letter to the Commissioner of Police with his interpretation of it:

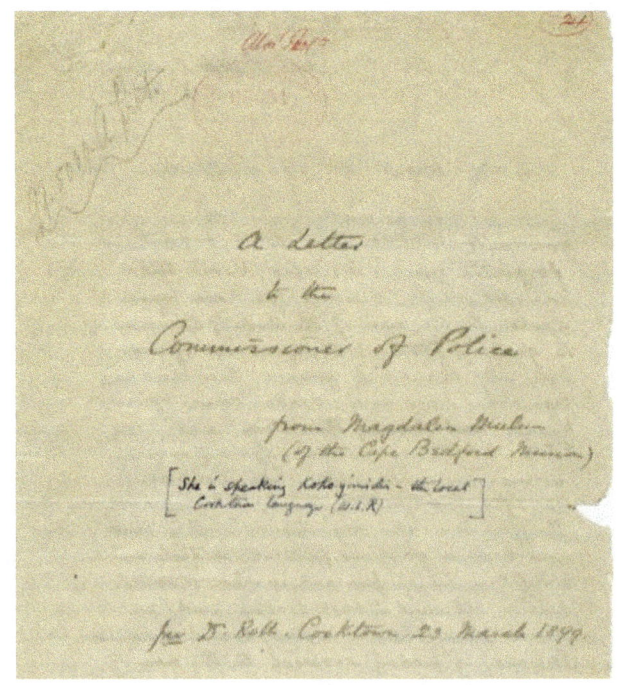

- A letter to the Commissioner of Police from Magdalen Mulun (of Cape Bedford Mission). {She is speaking Koko-yimidirr – the local Cooktown language (W.I.R.)}

> General Translation
>
> Cape Bedford – month of March.
>
> Our friend Mr. Parry O'Keden.
>
> We are now writing you a letter, by which you will certainly see that we have not forgotten you. We also know that down-below (i.e. in Brisbane) you have again spoken to the men-of-the-Queen (Government) to give us food. Therefore all of us
>
> Perhaps, by making-a-speech to the men-of-the-Queen (Government) you could obtain a boat for us? Our friend Dr Roth has also now come to see us: he is learning our language. We are sending this letter through him. We will forward you by-boat shortly (some) button-orchids on a tea-tree. All the other girls have ordered me to make-a-speech like this to you.
>
> Your friend Magdalen, (the) Quandong.

"Dora Gibson from Hope Vale provided further information on Magdalen who was from one of the well-known and influential families on Cape Bedford Mission. Magdalen was one of the most talented pupils at Elim School and became proficient in writing Guugu Yimithirr. She took a lead in the community and provided information to Roth on local knowledge, including language."

My objective in including this interaction between Dr Roth and Magdalen was to further illustrate a willingness to peacefully coexist through acceptance and understanding.

The Lutheran Missionaries at Cape Bedford Mission strove to preserve the local language and to convert it into text so that it could be utilized in both oral and written form. Since those times the Guugu Yimithirr people have continued the fight to preserve their culture and language and today the children at Hope Vale School are being taught this as part of the school curriculum.

Chapter 5

The Grandparents
Robert McAndrew

My first knowledge of Robert McAndrew was from the Yarrabah Baptism Records where he is named as the father of Tibby. In my later research, I found a Mrs Gorton who also claimed this in her correspondence with government authorities. She stated that Tibby had been left in her care at infancy by her father Robert McAndrew. The role of the Gorton family in Tibby's life will be dealt with later.

In 2013 I enlisted help from the Cooktown Historical Society. A series of email conversations began between Marge Scully, a member of that society, and myself. She was able to furnish me with information about the Gorton family and also came up with the following:

{**From:** Historical Society
To: CECILY GRAY
Sent: Thursday, October 03, 2013 9:06 AM
Subject: Re: Sonata Cattle station Gorton family
Hi Cecily. The information re Robert McAndrew comes from the Cooktown Court House records, which we were able to access before they were sent to Brisbane. This might seem a bit strange seeing as he died in Mossman but all BDM records for the area where registered in Cooktown. }

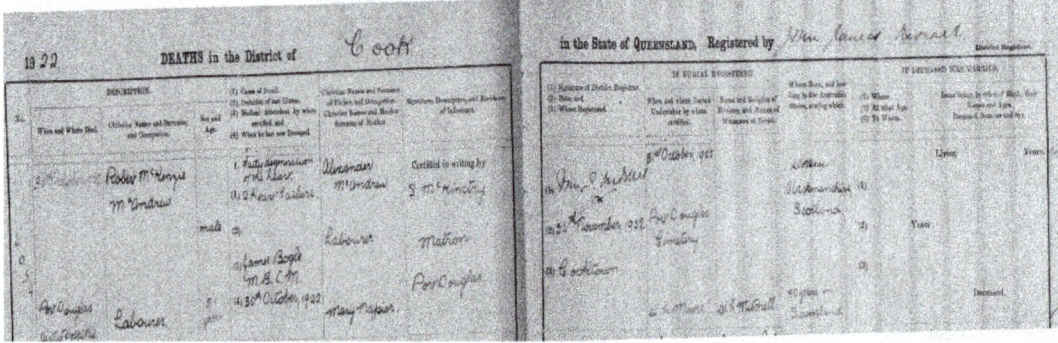

Cooktown Courthouse Records

The record has the following information:

- *{30th October 1922 – Port Douglas District Hospital*
- *Robert McAndrew – labourer – Male*
- *Cause of Death - Heart Failure*
- *Father – Alexander McAndrew – labourer.*
- *Mother – Mary Napier. Clackmannanshire Scotland.*
- *30 years in Queensland}*
- *Robert's father died in Dollar Clackmannanshire:*

Cook memorial 2011

By way of a DNA search through "**Ancestry.Com**", a family connection to a client "A. M." was discovered'.

- *"A close look at the family tree of my "High confidence of a 4-6th cousin relationship" match, "A.M", found that their great-great-great grandmother was the sister of Alexander McAndrew. Alexander's son was Robert McAndrew, whose details match with a Robert McAndrew who came to Queensland in 1889.*
- *A passenger list and a death notice for him that mostly match – middle names are different but the comparison below indicates that they are the one and same person.*

Robert McAndrew – Record Detail Matches			
	"A.M." Family Tree	Passenger List – from London to Brisbane, 24 May 1889 (QLD Passenger Lists 1848 – 1912	Death Notice (1922, QLD)
Name	Robert Drysdale McAndrew	Robert McAndrew	Robert McKenzie McAndrew
Birth Year	About 1866	About 1867	Not stated
Birth Place	Dollar, Clackmannanshire, Scotland	Clackmanna (typo?)	Not stated
Parents	Alexander McAndrew 22 Apr 1827 Collessie, Fife, Scotland Mary Napier about 1831 Stirling, Stirlingshire, Scotland	Not stated	Alexander McAndrew Mary Napier

- *It's interesting that all of "A.M."'S family throughout the generations are Scottish – born, lived and died there except for Robert and his brother James who died in Canada in 1916.}"[8]*

This analysis corresponded with the information I had obtained from Marge Scully at the Cooktown Historical Society. (NB. The Port Douglas District Hospital is situated at Mossman NQ)
Marge Scully revealed that he was employed at a cattle station 'Strathleven' near Mossman just prior to his death in 1922.
In summary, it seems that Robert McAndrew was probably born at the town of Dollar in the Clackmannan Shire, Scotland in 1866. He arrived in Brisbane, Australia at age about 23.
During the 1890s he was most likely employed on the Sonata cattle station at McIvor near Cooktown. Sometime after 1896, he placed his daughter Tibby (the result of a relationship with Maggie) in the care of Mrs Marion Gorton, wife of the station owner. It is most likely that he left to go in search of work.

---

[8] *Analysis by my niece, Deborah in 2019*

In 1922 at age about 56, he fell ill while employed at Strathleven station near Mossman North Queensland. He suffered a heart attack and passed away in the Port Douglas District Hospital on 30th October 1922.

> **These photographs show:**
> - The position of the town of Dollar in Scotland
> - A typical stone house to be found at Dollar
> - Castle Campbell one time residence of Mary Queen of Scots near Dollar township today
> - The town of Dollar this century

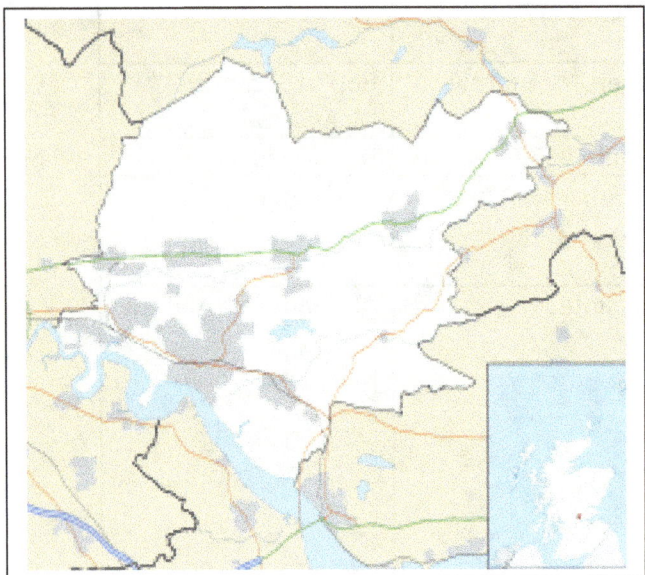

Chapter 6
Tibby McAndrew

In the Baptism Register it is recorded that Tibby came from Cooktown. My research has found that as a child she lived on a cattle station "Sonata" outside of Cooktown. As too, her mother Maggie.

This station was owned by William Vernon Gorton (1853-1929) and his wife Marion (nee Chapman 1855-?) On reading through the following archival records it can be established that Tibby had been placed in the care of Mrs Gorton by her father, Robert McAndrew (1866-1922). [9]

It was the historical practice to 'remove' light skinned children into the care of the Aboriginal Protector. This meant being placed on a Mission or Government Reserve. The need was seen as particularly relevant for girls nearing puberty. The intention was to protect them from seduction by white males, the practice of which was very prevalent at the time. The birth mothers would have had no say in the matter of their daughter's displacement.

In 1904 a real drama took place when the Protector tried to remove Tibby from Sonata. This was vehemently opposed by the station owner's wife Marion Gorton who wished to keep her.

Following are copies of actual 1904 archival records of the series of correspondence passed between Chief Protector <u>Walter Roth</u>, Nth Qld Protector <u>James King</u>, the (anonymous) <u>Undersecretary to the Minister</u> for Lands, Sergeant <u>John Kenny</u> of the Native Police, and <u>Mrs Marion Gorton</u> regarding eight year-old <u>Tibby</u>.

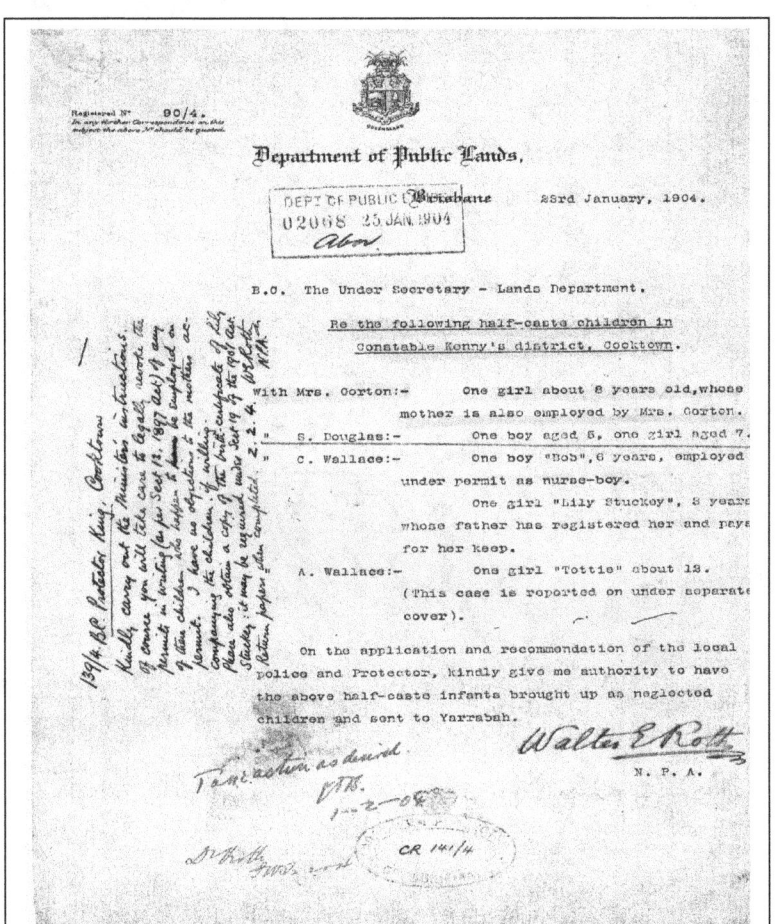

The <u>Undersecretary</u> issues orders to Protector <u>King</u> to round up the half caste children living on the nearby stations.

He gives attention to <u>Mrs Gorton</u> who is responsible for "one girl about 8 years old, whose mother is also employed by Mrs Gorton.

(Whether Tibby should have been classed as 'employable' later becomes a subject of contention)

---

[9] *(A/5875, 04/891, Report of 'Half-Caste' Children, re Tibby McAndrew)*

The contents of this document:

1. The Lands Department Undersecretary's order for Roth to send half-caste children to Yarrabah. This included: "With Mrs Gorton- One girl about 8 years old, whose mother is also employed by Mrs Gorton".
2. Roth's addendum forwarded to Protector King Cooktown. "Kindly carry out the Minister's instructions. Of course you will take care to legally revoke the permits in writing (as per Sect 12.1897 Act) of any of these children who happen to be employed on permit. I have no objections to the mothers accompanying the children, if willing. Please also obtain a copy of the birth certificate of Lily Stuckey. It may be required under Sect 19 of the 1901 Act. Return papers when completed.2.2.4. W E Roth NPA

On receiving notice of this intention to remove Tibby, Mrs Gorton then endeavours to intervene by writing directly to Dr Roth. It seems they were socially acquainted. She writes:

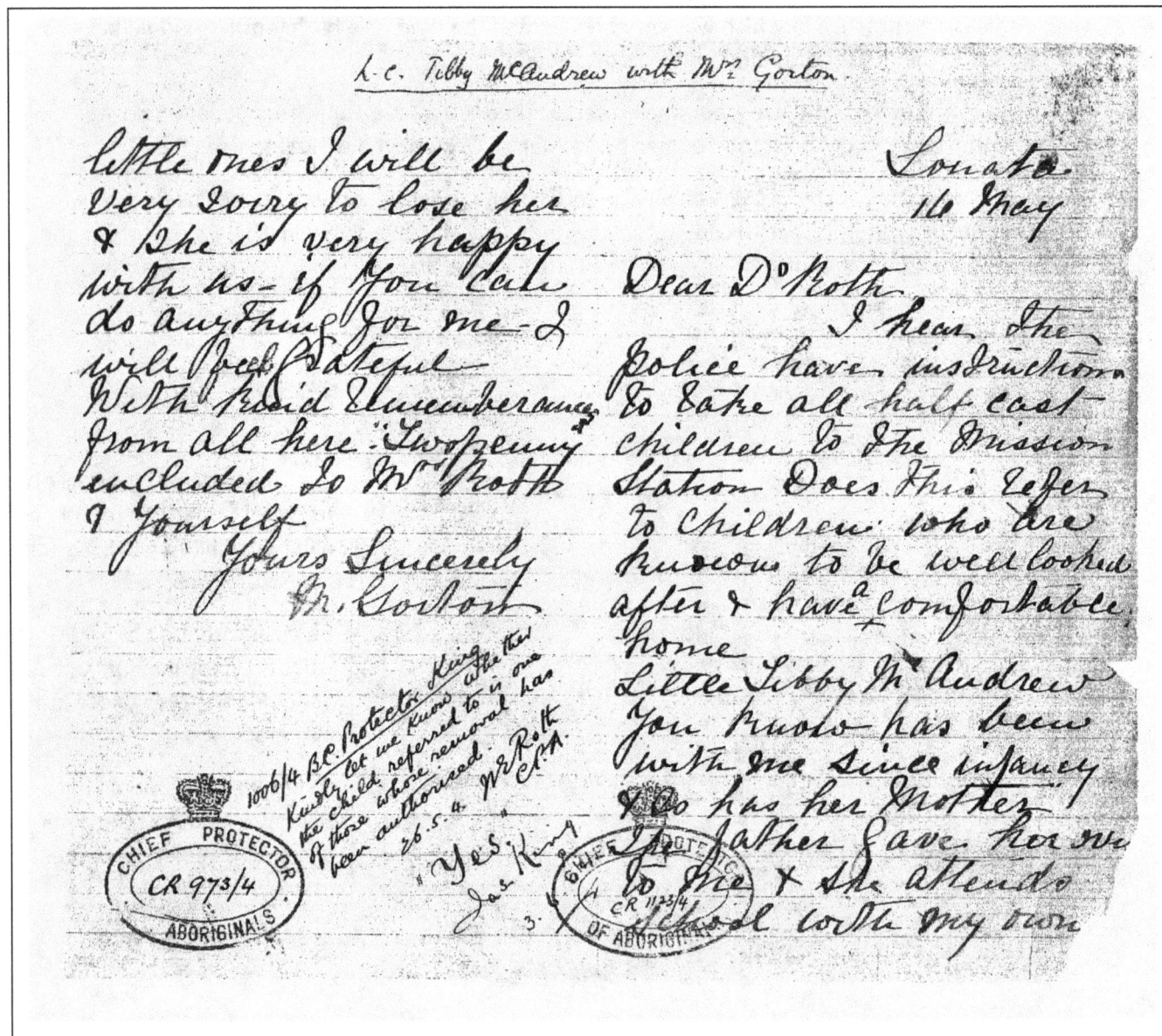

Sonata

- *Dear Dr Roth,* *16 May*
- *I hear the police have instructions to take all half cast children to the Mission Station. Does this refer to children who are known to be well looked after and have a comfortable home. Little Tibby McAndrew has been with me since infancy and so has her mother. The father gave her over to me and she attends school with my own little ones. I will be very sorry to lose her and she is very happy with us- if you can do anything for me I will feel grateful.*

With kind remembrance from all here. "Twopenny"* included to Mrs Roth and yourself.

Yours sincerely

M Gorton

*(Probably a small type of magazine)

Mrs Gorton included in her letter, an example of Tibby's literary ability which is of a good standard for any eight year-old. (Perhaps the recipient of Tibby's letter is her mother, "Maggie")

Sonata

My dear Maggie,

I hope you are quite well. Thank you very much for the lollies you sent. Minnie and I kept them for a long time and just eat a few each day. Mary Ann is up staying here and her and Minnie sleep down in your humpy now. We felt very lonely when you first went but now we are used to it. Ruby and Jack are leaving in the morning so we will be quite (quiet) again. The garden is nice now plenty of tomatoes and pumpkins

Walter Roth's acknowledgement of receipt of Mrs Gorton's letter:

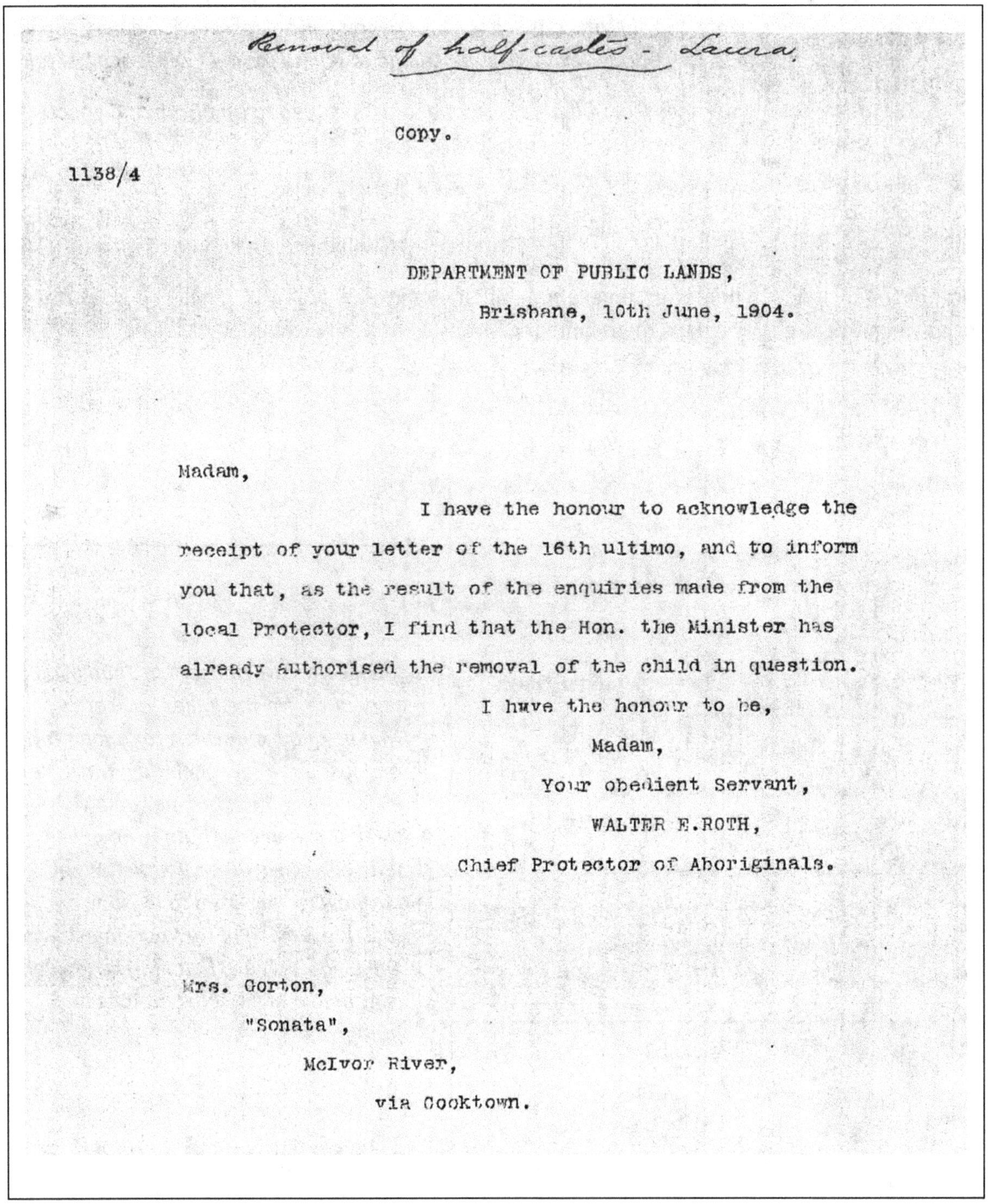

Removal of half-castes – Laura.

Copy.

1138/4

DEPARTMENT OF PUBLIC LANDS,
Brisbane, 10th June, 1904.

Madam,

I have the honour to acknowledge the receipt of your letter of the 16th ultimo, and to inform you that, as the result of the enquiries made from the local Protector, I find that the Hon. the Minister has already authorised the removal of the child in question.

I have the honour to be,
Madam,
Your obedient Servant,
WALTER E. ROTH,
Chief Protector of Aboriginals.

Mrs. Gorton,
"Sonata",
McIvor River,
via Cooktown.

"Madam,
- I have the honour to acknowledge the receipt of your letter of the 16th ultimo, and to inform you that, as the result of enquiries made from the local Protector, I find that the Hon. the Minister has already authorised the removal of the child in question."

It seems that Mrs Gorton, having known Dr Roth socially, went directly to him with her request to keep Tibby. Obviously Roth could not openly interfere with the authorisations of the Minister. However Mrs Gorton had put the cat among the pigeons and as can be seen in the following document, the efforts then made to allow Tibby to remain with Mrs Gorton…

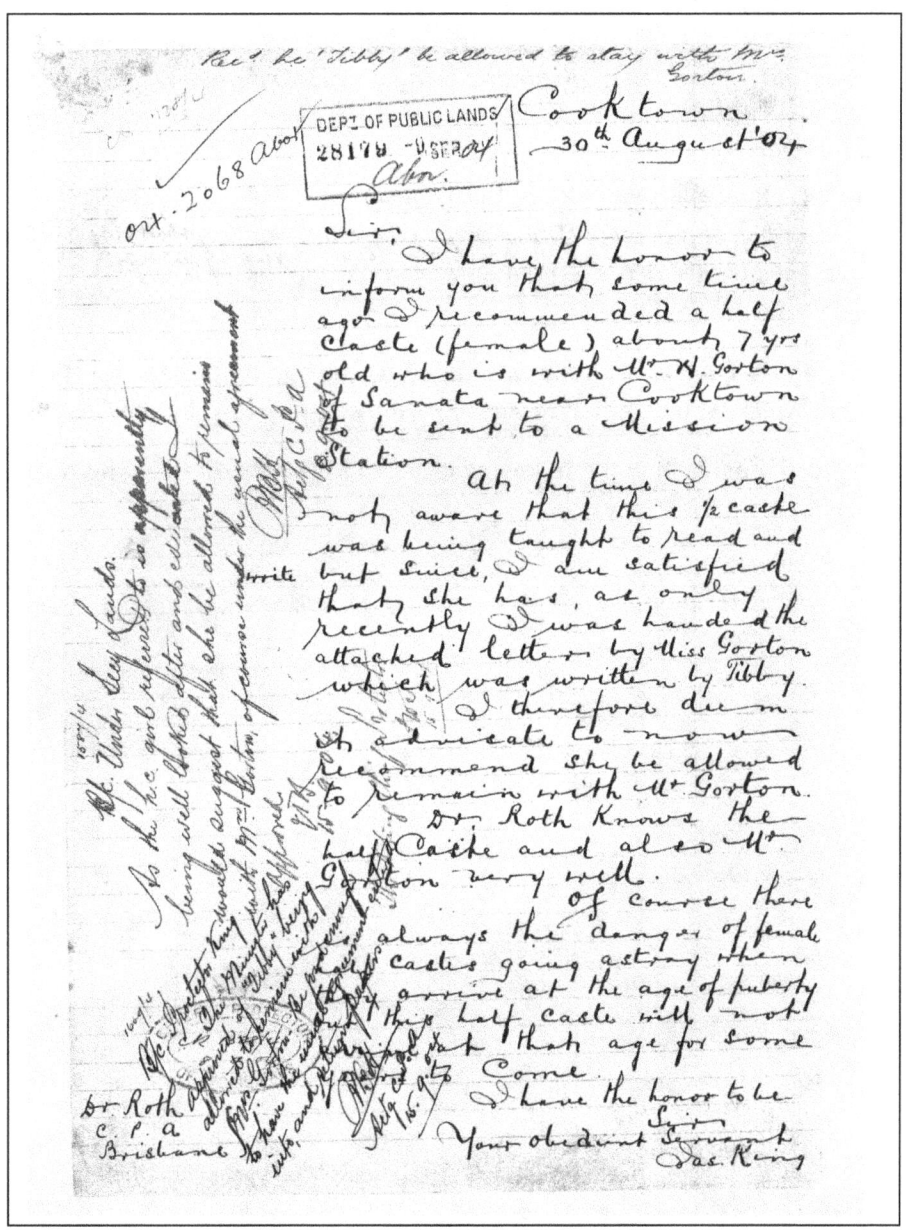

The document shows:

1. The original letter from King to Under Sec Lands explaining that he was unaware of Tibby's situation with the Gorton family 30th August 1904:
- "I have the honour to inform you that, some time ago I recommended a half caste (female) about 7 years old who is with Mrs M Gorton of Sonata near Cooktown to be sent to a Mission Station. At the time I was not aware that this ½ caste was being taught to read and write but since, I am satisfied that she has as only recently I was handed the attached letter by Mrs Gorton which was written by Tibby. I therefore deem it advisable to now recommend she be allowed to remain with Mrs Gorton."

> *Dr Roth knows the half caste and also Mrs Gorton very well. Of course there is always the danger of female half-castes going astray when they arrive at the age of puberty and this half-caste will not arrive at that age for some time to come. I have the honour to be signed, your obedient servant, James King."*

2. An addendum by the <u>Undersecretary to the Minister</u> to <u>Roth</u> approving procedures to progress.

- *"As the h.c. girl referred to is apparently being well looked and educated I would suggest that she be allowed to remain with Mrs Gorton, of course under the usual agreement. "* (September 1904)

3. Addendum: A final approval from <u>Roth to King</u>,

- *"The minister has approved of 'Tibby' being allowed to remain with Mrs Gorton. Be good enough to have the usual agreement entered into, and return papers".(15th September 1904)*

The Gortons would have been very happy with the outcome had it not been for the proviso of a written agreement which would demand wages for Tibby be provided by the Gortons.

<u>Mr Gorton</u> henceforth despatched the following letter to <u>Mr King</u> expressing his displeasure at the idea of having to pay wages to Tibby:

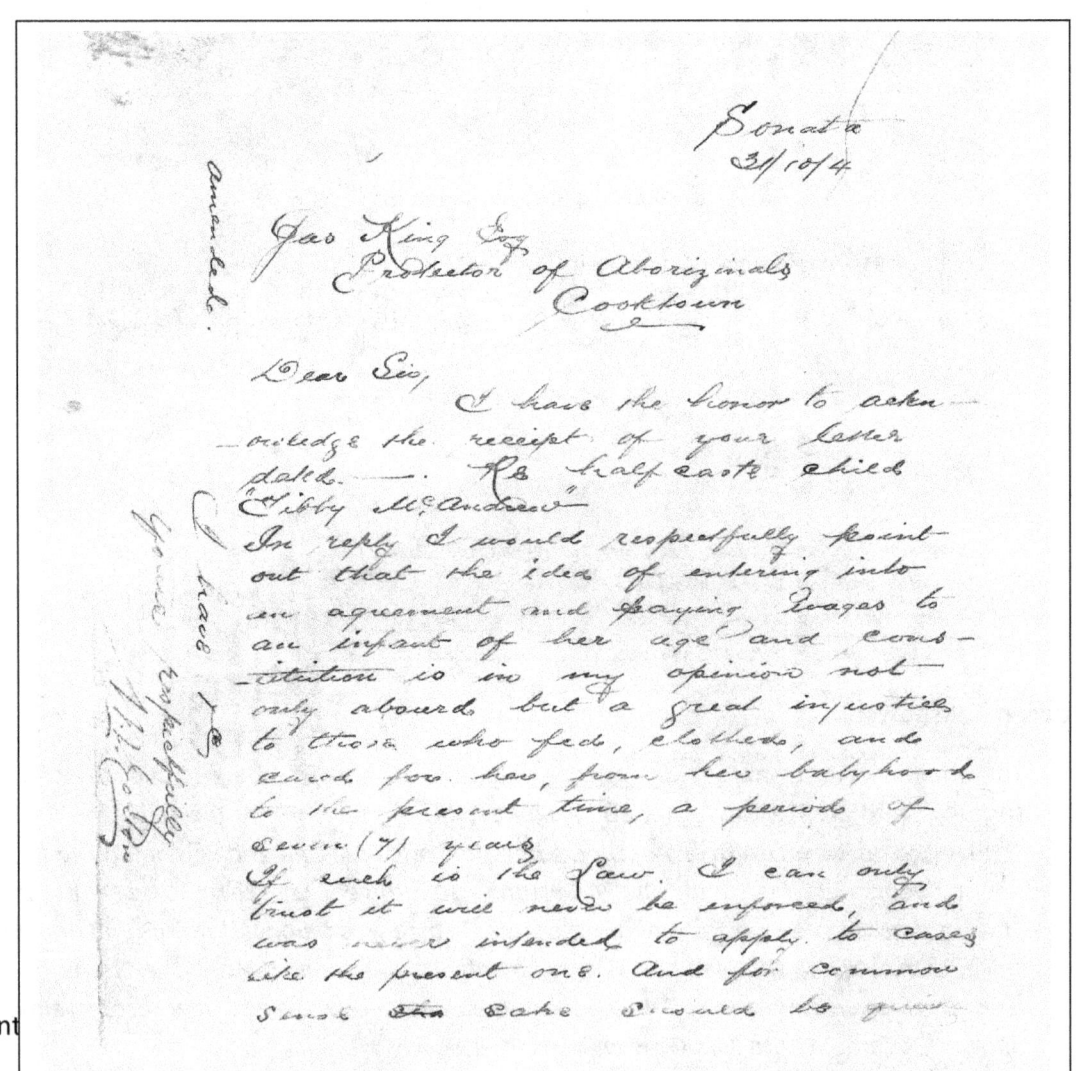

The cont

- *"I have the honour to acknowledge receipt of your letter dated_____. Re half caste girl Tibby McAndrew.*

  In reply I would especially point out that the idea of entering into an agreement and paying wages to an infant of her age and condition is in my opinion not only absurd but a great injustice to those who fed, clothed and cared for her, from her babyhood to the present time, a period of seven (7) years. If such is the law, I can only trust it will never be enforced, and was never intended to apply to cases like the present one. And for common sense sake should be greatly amended."

On the 5th November 1904 <u>King</u> forwards this letter to <u>Roth</u> with Mr Gorton's letter attached;

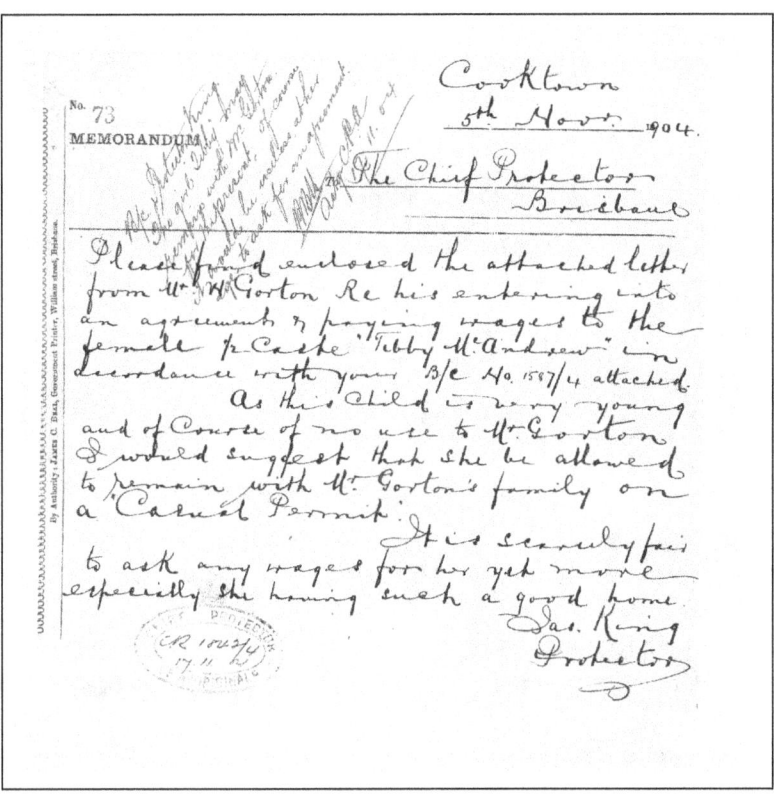

The contents of this document are:

1. 5th November 1904 <u>King to Roth</u>:
- *Please find enclosed letter from Mr Gorton re his entering into an agreement and paying wages to the female ½ caste "Tibby McAndrew" in accordance with your B/C No.1587/4 attached. As this child is very young and of course of no use to Mr Gorton I would suggest that she be allowed to remain with Mr Gorton's family on a Casual Permit. It is scarcely fair to ask any wages for her yet more especially she having such a good home.*
2. 17th November <u>Roth's</u> addendum to <u>King's</u> letter:
- *The girl Tibby may remain with Mr Gorton for the present. Of course it would be useless at her age to ask for an agreement.*

<u>In February 1905, Roth is still chasing up the papers concerning Tibby's employment.</u>

<u>King responds</u> as he had obviously received Mr Gorton's letter and passed it on.

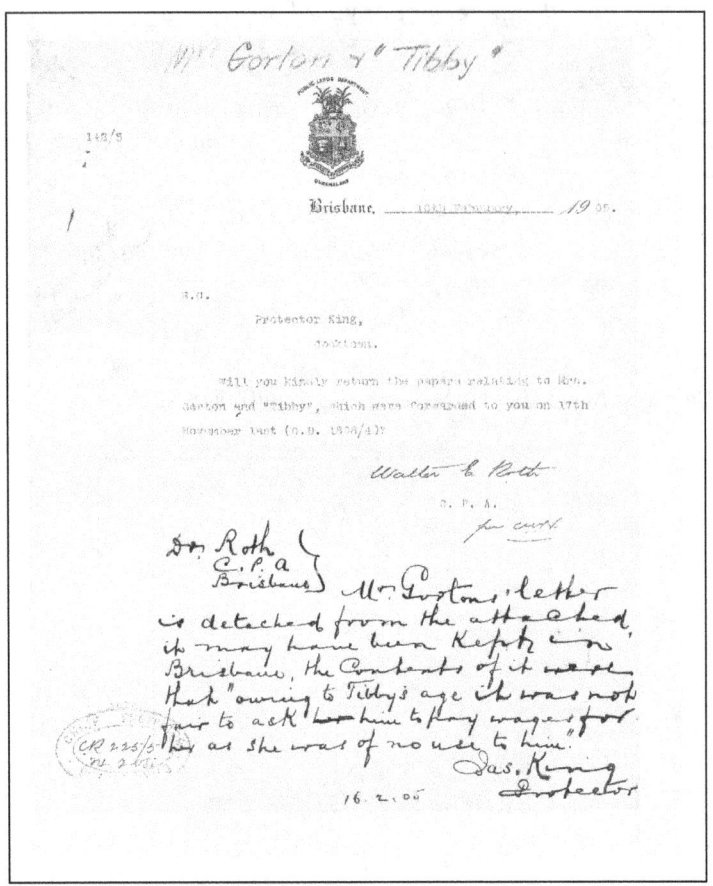

This document contains:

1. 10th Feb 1905 Roth to King:
- "Will you kindly return the papers relating to Mrs Gorton and "Tibby" which were forwarded to you on 17th November last?"
2. 16 Feb 1905 addendum King to Roth,
- "Mrs Gorton's letter is detached from the attached, it may have been kept in Brisbane, the contents of it were that "owing to Tibby's age it was not fair to ask (her) him to pay wages for her as she was of no use to him"

Apparently the previous letter 5th November from King had been overlooked by Roth. His acknowledgement of it is dated 17th November 1904.

So it seems the status quo returned to Sonata with Tibby remaining and the Gortons off the hook in regard to payment of wages.

I can only imagine John King's concerns for Tibby's vulnerability on reaching puberty were not unfounded and perhaps even prophetic because in six short years, she would find herself abandoned by all she loved and "Stolen" far away – a child, with a child growing inside her, torn from the life she knew and forced into another of virtual imprisonment. I can only imagine the heartbreak felt by the woman who had stood firm for her and fought tooth and nail to keep her back then in 1904, but <u>on 29 November 1910 Tibby was "removed from Cooktown to Yarrabah Mission Cairns as she is in the family way"</u>

I have mentioned the role that the Cape Bedford mission played in the lives of the Guugu Yimithirr people to whom Tibby belonged.

It would have seemed logical for her to be been sent there instead of all the way to Yarrabah.

However, it was the philosophy of the German missionaries there that would have rejected any attempt to place her there.

"Schwarz was aiming at complete isolation of the residents from white settlement. He wanted to be able to offer work so that mission residents were not lured into town or to work on the luggers, where he said they gained not civilization but "syphilization". Actually the mission was free from syphilis – a remarkable exception.

Schwarz also refused to accept "waifs" or "strays" or offenders, work absconders or "morally destitute" Aborigines which the government might want to allocate to the mission, arguing that it was not a reformatory.

He refused to be recruited into government service through the money available to missions that were declared reformatories."[10]

So I guess in the eyes of Schwarz, Tibby would have met a few of his criterion for rejection.

George Schwarz (1868 – 1959)

Ant hill at Cape Bedford

---

[10] *German Missionaries in Australia. Cape Bedford Mission (Hope Vale) (1886-1942) – Regina Ganter Griffith University*

Removals Register January 1911[11]

Tibby arrived at Yarrabah in January 1911 and her daughter, Gladys was born 6th February 1911.

As mentioned earlier, they were both baptised in St Albans Anglican Church Yarrabah in November 1911

Also on 28th November 1911 Tibby McAndrew married Samuel Myquick at St Albans church Yarrabah. One of Tibby's granddaughters was to tell me that Tibby had said, 'They married me off to an old man'. She might well have been justified in saying this, given that Sam's eldest child left back on Badu Island was just 1 year younger than Tibby. Without having an exact birth date, it's impossible to know Sam's age at the time but he would have been considerably older than the 15 year old Tibby.

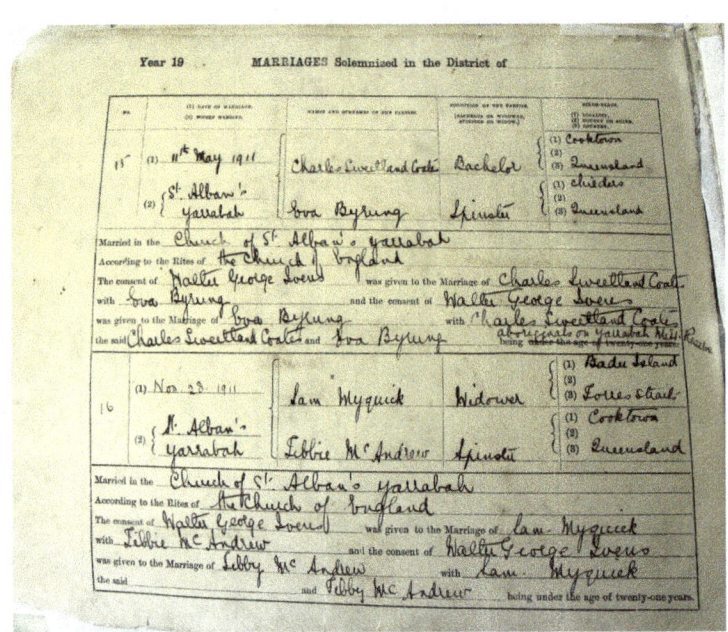

---

[11] *QSA Item ID 302738, A/58995, 1910/2117 Miscellaneous, letter dated 29 November 1910 from Protector of Aboriginal Cooktown – That Tibby McAndrew half caste in the employ of Mrs Gorton be sent to Yarrabah as she is in the family way.*

Chapter 7
Samuel Myquick

Although not by blood, culturally Sam Myquick is considered to be my grandfather. As recorded in the Aboriginal News, Samuel arrived at Yarrabah in May 1907. He is said to have come from Badu Island in the Torres Strait.

By 1907, Ernest Gribble had really made his mark on the Yarrabah Mission. One of his many innovations was the establishment of a regular newspaper, "The Aboriginal News".

Samuel Myquick's arrival at Yarrabah is recorded in the edition below:

THE ABORIGINAL NEWS

$1 Per annum posted   Printed at Yarrabah

VOL. II. NO. 7.   Registered at the G P O Brisbane for transmission by post as a news paper.   MAY 15, 1907

Church of England Mission to Australian Aboriginals

"Lift up thy prayer for the remnant that is left"

AIMS

1. The evangelization and elevation of the Aboriginals by preaching the Gospel, and teaching them habits of industry.
2. It is believed this can be done by (a) Gathering them into communities surrounding them with Christian influence and protecting them from evils too often associated with European service.
(b) By getting them to take an interest in themselves as a people and cultivating self-respect.

Yarrabah
Founded June 17 1892

Postal Adress
Cairns Queensland

STAFF
Rev. E R Gribble   Mrs E. R. Gribble
                Mrs. J. B. Gribble
Mr L Woolrych   Mrs. L. Woolrych
Mr. B. S Cole   Mrs. W. Reeves
Mr. D.H.T. Gosper   Miss Monaghan
Mr. H. Wriece
Mr. W. Abbrym
Mr A. Obah
Hon. worker Miss Gribble

Trubanaman
Founded June 1 1905

Postal Address
Mitchell River
Normanton

STAFF
Mr. ... Matthews
Mr T. A. Williams
Mr. J. De. Le. Perelle
Mr. Bob. Ling

Yarrabah Brass Band

Aboriginal Lay Readers licensed by the Bishop of the Diocese

James Noble   Philip Meringhee
Richard Yimbungni   Alick Bybee
Clement

It reads; "New Arrival. From the Island of Badu we have admitted a man by name Myquick. So far he has proved a good fellow his work being well done and his conduct very good"[12]

---

[12] *Aboriginals-Missions A/70007, Folder: Aboriginal News, Yarrabah, April 1906 to August 1907), admission of Sam Myquick from Badu Island A/69468, Aboriginals-Yarrabah, List of Marriageable Men and boys at Yarrabah, mentions Myquick Torres Strait Islander*

During Easter of 1907 Sam was removed from Badu Island to Yarrabah Mission via Thursday Island.

It's not clear why he was removed but apparently he was involved in something that the authorities wanted kept quiet. A letter to the Chief Protector from the Government Resident at Thursday Island said in relation to this removal:

- " re Badu crime consider desirable avoid publicity endorse Protector's view deportation".[13]

Some History of Badu Island:

Badu: aka (Mulgrave Island) is an island 60km north of Thursday Island in the Torres Strait. Badu Island once had a feared reputation as an island of head-hunters. Warfare, turtle and dugong hunting were the main occupations of Badu men until the 1870s with the turtle and dugong hunting continuing after this. Pearlers established bases on the island during the1870s, and by 1880s, the islanders depended on wages earned as lugger crew. At the same time, the first missionaries arrived.

Captain William Bligh, in charge of the British Naval ships Providence and Assistant, visited the Torres Strait in1792 and mapped the main reefs and channels. While sailing between Badu and Jervis islands, Bligh's crew fired a volley of shots of warning after they observed a number of canoes approaching these ships from Badu. It was then that Bligh named the Island Mulgrave…….

Torres Strait Islanders refer to the arrival of the London Missionary Society (LMS) missionaries at Erub (a nearby island also known as Darnley) in July 1871 as "the Coming of the Light". The LMS had made unsuccessful efforts to place missionary teachers on Badu in the 1870s. In 1884 the people of Badu made contact with the LMS mission at Jervis Island and informed them they were now ready to receive missionaries……[14]

The Queensland Government over time began to exert more influence on the lives of Torres Strait Islander people. John Douglas, the Government Resident at Thursday Island, initially shielded Torres Strait Islanders from the controlling provisions of the *Aboriginal Protection and Restriction of the Sale of Opium Act 1897*. After Douglas passed away in 1904, the administration that followed began to assert control over Torres Strait Islander labour and savings accounts and imposed restrictions on Islander movement to and from the Mainland.[15]

Sam was somehow implicated in an incident on Badu. His hasty removal first to Thursday Island to avoid scandal probably means that one or more white residents were also involved. This is something that will never be known for sure but in situations such as this, it was usually the natives who lost out.

---

[13] *Item ID 89689, Chief Protectors Inwards Correspondence Register 1907-1909, Government Resident, 07/382, letter re removal of Myquick from Badu Island*

[14] *Torres Strait Regional Council website*
[15] *Queensland Government home for Queenslanders Aboriginal and Torres Strait Islander peoples Cultural awareness, heritage and the arts. Aboriginal and Torres Strait Islander community histories. Communities A-B Badu*

When he left Badu, Sam was a widower with four children, two sons (Danalgub Maikuik – born 1897 and Sam Hosea born 1899) and two daughters (Kaka Maikuk born 1901 and Luna Maikuk born 1903).These children were left on the island. He was never to return to the island.[16]

Sam's brother Nomoa adopted the children and raised them with his own. "Departmental records indicate that in 1921 Nomoa was living on Badu Island and was 'old and almost blind'. He had a wife and five children. He also had three adopted children……." [17]

The following photographs are from an *Album of views of the Torres Strait Islands Queensland ca 1928-1929/Charles Maurice Yonge*

Village Badu Island Torres Strait Queensland

---

[16] *(Anna Shnukal Genealogy of the Maikuk family)*
[17] *(A/58756, 21/1477, Islands, Torres Strait 1921, re pension for Nomoa of Badu Island)*

Villagers platting the leaves from the coconut palms, Badu Island. Queensland ca 1928

Hut wall constructed of platted leaves from coconut palms ca 1928

Chapter 8

Hull River Settlement

On 6th May 1915 Sam, Tibby and their two children were removed to Hull River Mission. [18]

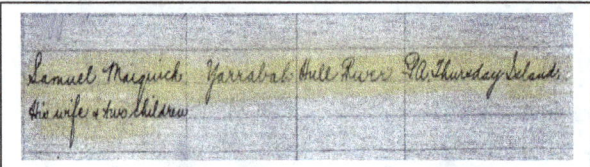 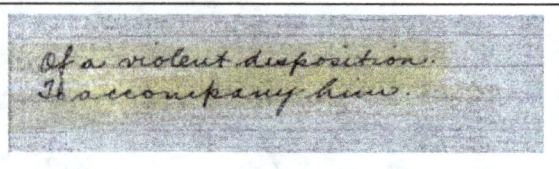

Samuel Myquick – Yarrabah – Hull River – PA. Thursday Island – Of a violent disposition

His wife and two children to accompany him

Tibby and Sam are named as parents of:

- Maria Mercy, born 12th May 1913 or 1914 at Yarrabah. (Maria was later married to Tom Callope.) Her father was Sam Myquick. [19]
- Elizabeth, born 14th September 1917 at Innisfail. [20]

Elizabeth was married to Robert Footscray at Mapoon on 3rd February 1932. Her father was Sam Myquick. [21]

The two children who went to Hull River from Yarrabah, were four year old Gladys and two year old Maria. Elizabeth was born later (1917) at the Hull River Settlement.

The settlement at Hull River is mistakenly called a "mission". A mission has a religious involvement. This was not so at the Hull River Settlement. It was established by the Queensland Government in 1914 as a place to help settle social problems caused by a clash of cultures between the local Djiru people and the European settlers. Although named "Hull River", it was actually established on the beach (now known as South Mission Beach) north of the mouth of the Hull River with the river flowing southward west of the site.

John Martin Kenny, the same non-commissioned Native Police Officer who was involved in the attempted removal of Tibby from Sonata in 1904, was promoted to be Superintendent at Hull River and arrived on 1st September 1914. He had come from Cooktown where he had been employed as an engineer and overseer at Cape Bedford Mission.

He set about establishing the settlement questionably choosing a site which was exposed to the onshore winds. Homes were built for the families of the Superintendent, Assistant superintendent and store keeper, and a school. The other residents were housed mainly along the seafront in dwellings made of ti-tree bark.

---

[18] (A/64785, Removals Register, 1915 entry for Sam and Tibby Myquick and their children.
[19] Anna Shnukal genealogy of the Myquick family
[20] (Palm Island Social History Card for Elizabeth Footscray; Queensland death for Elizabeth Bethel Dallachy, no.1999/56966).
[21] (Anna Scnukal genealogy of the Myquick family; Queensland marriage certificate for Robert Footscray and Elizabeth Myquick, no. 1932/C739)

Food provision was very basic so it was necessary to supplement this with bush tucker, fishing and when a boat was available, turtle hunting. The people worked mostly on the settlement growing bananas and other crops but were sometimes employed by land owners in the near district.

Site of Hull River Settlement Bingil Bay 1902

The population grew as "removals" arrived from other areas, placed there for "disciplinary reasons for their relief and protection".

By 1916 there were about 490 residents but by March 1918 there were only 300. Many had succumbed to the malaria epidemic which swept through the settlement in 1917 and others had deserted when they could. [22]

---

[22] *"Indigenous History" (http://www.cassowaryconservation.asn.au/indigenous-history.html). Community for Coastal and Cassowary Conservation, 10 March 1918. Retrieved 26 February 2020*

The site of the settlement in 2011 looking south towards Hull Heads

It was here, in May 1915 that Tibby would once again cross paths with John Kenny, now the Superintendent of Hull River Settlement but perhaps neither were aware of their previous connection.

Aboriginal people at the Hull River Settlement (the "Mission") in 1916

(Photo courtesy John Oxley Library) More than likely, the Myquick family are in this photograph but the image is too unclear to distinguish individuals.

Life was now much more difficult than it had been while under the supervision of the Anglican Church back at Yarrabah. As well as the lack of physical provisions, their spiritual wellbeing had also taken a setback.

It seems that Samuel Myquick endeavoured at least to overcome the spiritual shortfall by rallying the residents to practice their Christian faith and conducting regular services. The following is a letter he despatched to the Protector asking for assistance with that:[23]

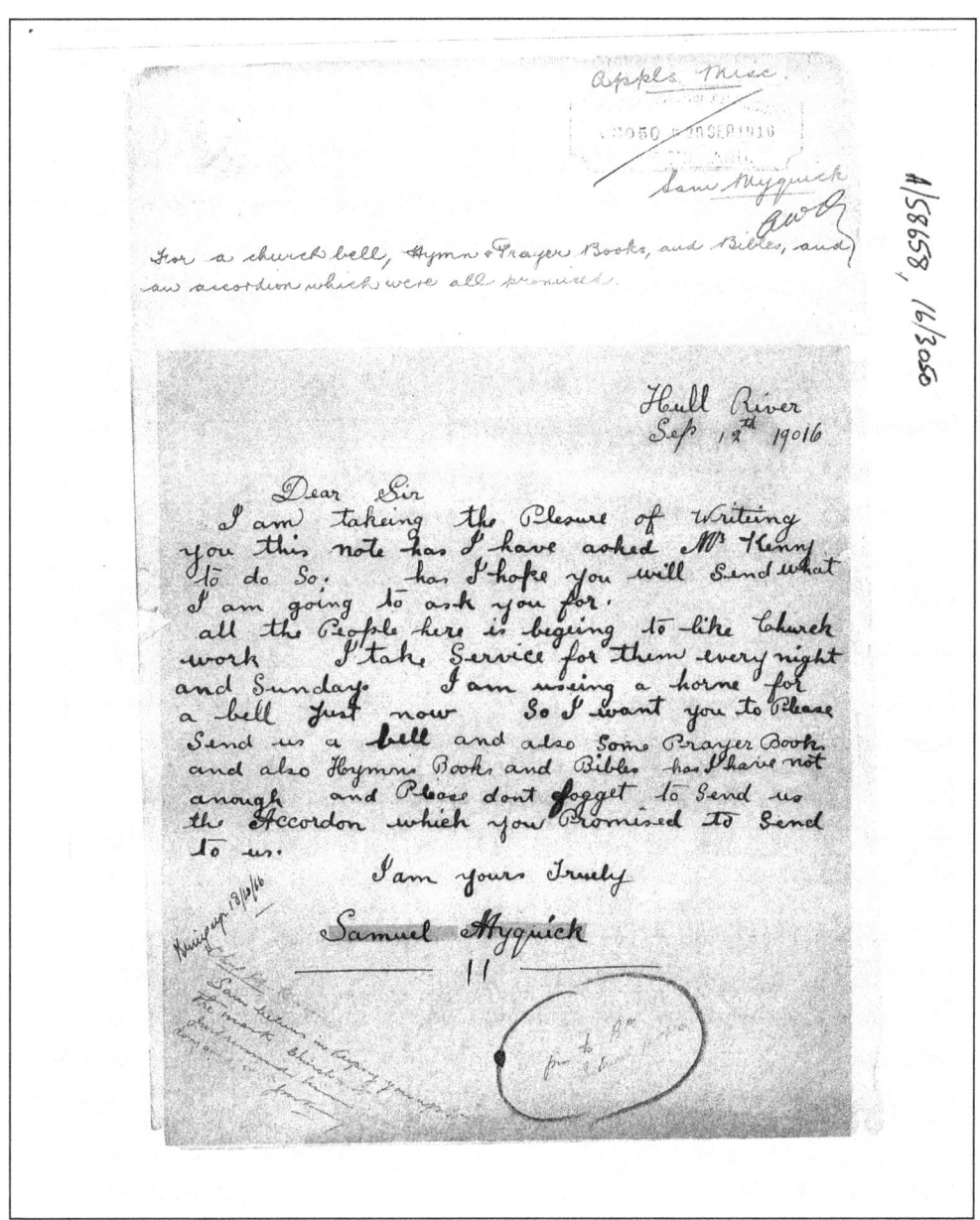

Sam writes in his letter to the Chief Protector Brisbane:

---

[23] *Chief Protector of Aboriginals inward correspondence register. A/58658,16/3050*

Hull River

Sep 12th 1916

- *Dear Sir*

I am taking the pleasure of writing you this note (h) as I have asked Mr Kenny to do so. (h) as I hope you will send what I am going to ask for.

All the people here is beginning to like church work. I take Service for them every night and Sunday. I am using a horn for a bell just now so I want you to please send us a bell and also some Prayer Books and also Hymn Books and Bibles as I have not enough and please don't forget to send us the accordion which you promised to send to us.

I am yours truly

Samuel Myquick

Superintendent Kenny writes this addendum:

- *Chief P.A. Brisbane*

Sam believes in keeping you up to the mark Churchman. Please just remind him that he's doing good work.

John Kenny   (Pin to Prot. instruction papers)

For a church bell, Hymn and Prayer Books, and Bibles, and an accordion, which were all promised.

It is on record that Sam was removed to Hull River because of his "violent disposition". Yet on his arrival at Yarrabah, he is described as, 'a good fellow, his work being well done and his conduct good'.

As a child, Sam would have enjoyed the freedom of Badu Island. Law and order on the island would have been maintained according to tribal tradition. By the time Queensland Government intrusion began, he would have been a mature adult. So a person unused to this, would have had to make quite difficult adjustments to the way things were changing. However, it seems out of character for Sam to be described as violent. The incident resulting in his removal from Badu doesn't suggest that violence was involved.

.Earnest Gribble controlled Yarrabah in a very authoritarian, even regimental manner. It is understandable that this could cause problems among the residents if they felt they were being treated too harshly. Frustration can lead to angry clashes which would not have been tolerated in the Gribble regime. A lapse in discipline could lead to disaster for the mission.

At Hull River, Sam showed strong leadership in ensuring the people continued to enjoy the comfort of practising their religion even though it was a non-sectarian establishment. Maybe it was this fortitude that had gotten him into trouble at Yarrabah.

Samuel Myquick passed away in 10 September 1917 of heart failure following pneumonia:

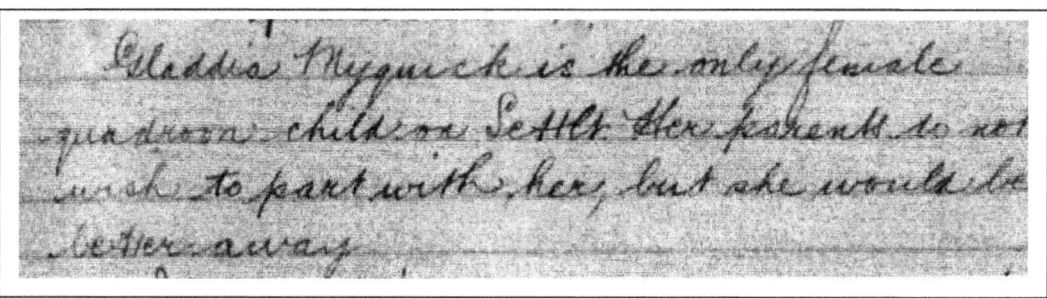

A curious entry found in the Hull River records:[24]

- *Gladdia Myquick is the only female quadroon child on the settlement. Her parents do not wish to part with her, but she would be better away.*

('Quadroon' was the name given to the child of a white person and a half-caste aborigine).

In fact though, Gladys was the child of a white father, (European Unknown) and 'quadroon' Tibby.

Tibby could have been classified 'quadroon', not 'half-caste' because she was the child of a white father (Robert McAndrew) and a half-caste (Maggie).

So to be accurate, Gladys's classification would be 'octoroon'.

Her paleness must have been very rare at the settlement. It is quite remarkable that Tibby was able to keep Gladys with her when so many other children were 'stolen' from their families.

---

[24] *A/58999, 16/1021, Hull River Misc.,*

Chapter 9
The Cyclone

On March 10 1918 a furious cyclone and tidal wave swept across the area and wiped out the Aboriginal settlement at Hull River, along with the homes and orchards of the scattered settlers on the coast. The afternoon the cyclone hit, a telephone link had been set up between Banyan (the forerunner of the Tully Township) and the "mission". It was not to be replaced for some time.

During the cyclone the camping area at the beach was covered to a depth of ten feet by the tidal wave which swept the bark and grass huts, and several people were also swept away and drowned. **Superintendent Kenny** and his daughter died, killed by flying debris, as did a number of Aboriginal people. Records show that 37 people were killed in Innisfail itself and a further 40-60 people killed in the surrounding area. It is likely that many more people were killed at the time. Record keeping was sketchy and it is possible that well over 100 people were, making it the worst natural disaster in Australia.[25]

My mother had told us of her experience in a horrific cyclone as a seven year old child. She described how they were all told to lie flat to the ground so the violent wind would not lift and carry them away. She told how branches, sheets of iron roofing and all sorts of other debris came flying over them as they lay saturated and terrified, clinging for life to the ground beneath them. She said many people were killed including some of the family of the people who were in charge of whatever the place was. (She was always vague about just where this had occurred)

On finding the records of the 1918 Hull River Cyclone in my research I was awestruck to realise that this was the one my mother had survived! The people she mentioned as having been killed, would have been **John Kenny** and his little daughter among very many others.

The remoteness of the settlement meant that it was days before the outside world was to learn the magnitude of the disaster. One may only imagine the horror of the situation facing the survivors as the storm finally subsided.

A rescue party set out on the 'Innisfail' from Townsville, reaching Dunk Island a few days later. They battled their way through the damaged vegetation and swollen rivers to get to the dead and injured people. The Mrs Kenny, pregnant at the time, was injured and sent to Townsville, but the Government Medical only arrived on March 31. The survivors who stayed at the settlement salvaged what food they could.[26]

---

[25] *"Indigenous History" (http://www.cassowaryconservation.asn.au/indigenous-history.html)*

[26] *"Indigenous History" (http://www.cassowaryconservation.asn/indigenous- history.html)*

The Government Medical Officer who arrived on March 31 tendered the following report to the Chief Protector:

Innisfail

4th April 1918

Sir,

I arrived per Government Ketch "Melbidir" at Hull River Settlement on Sunday the 31st instant, and remained until Tuesday April 2nd.

I found all the buildings flattened and widely dispersed but the Superintendent Mr Hazeldean had erected tent-like structures with timber and iron left, among these was a roomy Hospital.

I visited all the sick the first evening and told off those that required Hospital treatment. There were fifty or sixty others with minor troubles who attended next morning a Dispensary I established beside the Hospital building. I brought with me a considerable quantity of medicine that I believed would be useful under the circumstances that prevailed. I took five serious cases and placed them in comparative comfort in the Hospital and installed Nurse Thompson who came down with me from Innisfail, in charge, and classified what drugs the cyclone had not damaged beyond recognition in a small pharmacy within the Hospital building, then having organized a few assistants including Hospital orderlies. I again went around accompanied by Nurse Thompson and gave certain instructions regarding patients in their temporary homes (mostly females).

I found that the number of deaths amounted to nine including Kenny and his daughter. Of these four were killed outright and five died from exposure. All were buried before my arrival.

I have to mention admirable work accomplished by Mr Hazeldean and his wife as well as his assistants, the surviving members of the staff of administration and later on Mr Wright's valuable assistance before my arrival (back).

On Tuesday the 2nd April we left in an open boat (a flatty) to endeavour to intercept the "Kurandah" on her way north as the "Melbidir" had not turned up according to promise. I have to complain of unsailorlike conduct on the part of the "Kuranda" Captain who passed by well out to sea and would not see our signal until some passengers protested and I might say compelled him to turn back for us. (Mr Wright and myself). I came in for abundant abuse from the Captain who would not listen to neither explanation nor apology saying that he only turned back thinking there was really a person hurt or I suppose really deserving of rescue. We could not offer him any advertisement in that respect but as poor Officers endeavouring to accomplish a hard task, a perilous task, we hoped to get a more genial and sailorlike hospitality. I would ask for more protection from abuse in going about my work. I believe medical men may still maintain a certain amount of dignity and not lose that kindly consideration that obtains in private practice although <u>they are</u> engaged in Government Service and do hard duty on occasions.

I am   Sir

Yours very truly

Medical Officer Hull River

(Edward O'Leary)

To Mr Bleakley, Chief Protector of Aboriginals, South Brisbane, [27]

Innisfail
4th April 1918

Sir,

I arrived per Government Ketch "Melbidir" at Hull River Settlement on Sunday the 31st instant, and remained until tuesday April 2nd.

I found all the buildings flattened and widely dispersed but the Superintendent Mr Hazeldean had errected tent-like structures with timber and iron left, among these was a roomy Hospital.

I visited all the sick the first evening and told off those that required Hospital treatment. There were some fifty or sixty others with minor troubles who attended next morning a Dispensary I establish beside the Hospital building. I brought with me a considerable quantity of medicines that I believed would be useful under the circumstances that prevailed. I took in five serious cases and placed them in comparative comfort in the Hospital and installed Nurse Thompson who came down with me from Innisfail, in charge, and classified what drugs the Cyclone had not damaged beyond recognition in a small pharmacy within the Hospital building, then having organized a few assistants including Hospital orderlies. I again went around accompanied by Nurse Thompson and gave certain instructions regarding patients in their temporary homes (mostly females).

I found that the number of deaths amounted to nine including Mr Kenny and his daughter. Of these four were killed outright and five died from exposure. All were burried before my arrival.

I have to mention the admirable work accomplished by Mr Hazeldean and his wife as well as his assistants, the surviving members of the staff of administration and later on Mr Wright's valuable assistance before my arrival.

On tuesday the 2nd April we left in an open boat (a flatty) to endeavour to intercept the "Kurandah" on her way north as the "Melbidir" had not turned up according to promise. I have to complain of unsailorlike conduct on the part of the "Kurandah" Captain who passed by well out at sea and would not see our signal until some passenger protested and I might say compelled him to turn back for us. (Mr Wright and myself). I came in for abundant abuse from the Captain who would

not listen to neither explanation nor apology saying that he only turned back thinking there was really some person hurt or I suppose really deserving of rescue. We could not offer him any advertisement in that respect but as poor Officers endeavouring to accomplish a hard task, a perilous task, we hoped to get more genial and sailorlike hospitality. I would ask for more protection from abuse in going about my work. I believe medical men may still maintain a certain amount of dignity and not lose that kindly consideration that obtains in private practice although they are engaged in the Government Service and do hard duty on occasions.

I am
Sir
Yours very truly
Edward Leary
Medical Officer Hull River Settlement.

To
Mr Bleakley
Chief Protector of Aboriginals
SOUTH BRISBANE.

---

[27] *Chief Protector of Aboriginals inward correspondence register*

Mr Bleakley addressed the Medical Officer's complaint by forwarding the following letter to the manager of the shipping company operating "Kurandah".[28]

13th April. 1918

- Sir

I forward for your information an extract from the report of our Medical Officer for the Hull River Aboriginal Settlement opposite Dunk Island which explains itself.

These officers had been conducting relief operations at the station which was absolutely demolished by the cyclone and two officers and a number of natives killed and many injured and sick.

The Kuranda was their only hope of returning to Cairns without the loss of days, a serious thing as there was much other work of a similar kind awaiting their attention there also.

Yours obediently,

Chief Protector of Aboriginals

The Manager

A.U.S.N. Co.

---

[28] *Chief Protector of Aboriginals inward correspondence register*

Estimates of deaths varied, but it is probable that up to 10 Aboriginal people died and buried on the site, while Kenny and his daughter were buried in a separate location. Many people had fled into the bush, and many more may have died of their injuries.

The Government Health Inspector recommended the creation of a reserve on Great Palm Island, 37 miles (60km) off the coast north-east of Townsville to accommodate the remaining residents, and they along with other Aboriginal people rounded up by police in the surrounding bushland around Tully and Cardwell, were taken there forcibly from June 1918.The entire settlement was relocated to the new reserve, including salvageable building materials. After the settlement area was abandoned, white settlers slowly moved in, with a town being surveyed in 1938. Initially named Kenny, it was officially renamed as South Mission in 1967.[29]

The Mija Memorial, commemorating the victims of the cyclone, was unveiled 100 years later, on 10 March 2018 on the site of the old settlement.

Photographs taken of the Mija Monument on the old settlement site during my visit there in 2011 (This was prior to its further development and unveiling in 2018).

The commemorative plaque

The shelter housed the wall of information   **Dunk Island is in the distance**

---

[29] *"indigenous History"(http://www.cassowaryconservation.asn.au/indigenous-history.html*

Chapter 10
Dunk Island

Dunk Island has been mentioned several times. It lies 4km due east of the site of the Hull River Settlement and is often used as a location point for the settlement. It has an interesting history of its own.

Over the centuries it would have been decimated by one cyclone after another long before the one which raged through in 1918. Others have followed since, the most recent being 'Larry' 20th March 2006 and 'Yasi' 2nd February 2011.

Originally called Conanglebah, the island was home to the Bandjin and Djiru people. The first white settlers were Dr Edmund Banfield and wife, Bertha. His work as journalist and editor with the Townsville Bulletin had led to concerns for his health and well-being due to anxiety and exhaustion. They settled on the island in 1897 where the peace and tranquillity lead to a great recovery.

They lived off the bounty of the island combined with their chickens, cows and goats. This was occasionally supplemented with provisions delivered by boat from the mainland. They cleared four acres of land and planted fruit trees and vegetables. Fortified by much better health, he began to write a series of articles about his observations of the island using the pseudonym, Rob Krusoe.

His 1908 book 'The Confessions of a Beachcomber', was well received and he went on to write several others in his own name also.

My mother often spoke about the Banfields on Dunk Island so I think they must have been part of the local folklore at the settlement even at that time. One of the stories she told was of how, on the sudden death of Edmund, the elderly Bertha was left alone on the island with his body for several days before help arrived.

The Banfield House on Dunk Island ca. 1915

The following is an extract from a letter written by Dorothy Cottrell. In this, she recounts the circumstances of the death of Dr Banfield in 1923. Dorothy and her husband had been negotiating a purchase of several acres on Dunk Island at the time prior to Dr Banfield's death. They were friends with the Banfields and shared their love for the island.

A series of unusual and unforeseen circumstances occurred which caused the elderly Banfields to be left alone on the isalnd. A situation which caused no concern as they were used to a solitary life even though by this time there were usually others nearby on whom to rely in case of emergency.

Her letter illustrates her fondness for the Banfields and her distress at Edmund's passing.

- *" On Friday Mr Banfield said that he felt ill, but neither he nor Mrs Banfield were alarmed. But that night, he was in frightful agony and all Saturday morning, at midday he seemed better and told Mrs Banfield that he would try to sleep. A few minutes later he was dead. Mrs Banfield was alone with him until Tuesday when she sighted the Innisfail going south. She waved to them but Captain Baberhan (sic) thought that it was only a friendly greeting and went past the sandspit, but happening to turn he saw that Mrs Banfield had fainted on the beach. So he came back and the whole crew (all of whom were friends of the beachcomber's) attended the funeral. Mrs Banfield would not leave so one of the men stayed with her. No news reached us in Townsville until the Innisfail arrived then Mr Hopkins left at once and did the hundred and twenty miles in fifteen hours; Mrs Banfield was a little light headed at first, but is almost herself again now – brave little woman! The grief over the beachcomber's death was astounding, he was beloved by all classes and condition of men, and Mrs Banfield is being deluged by letters of sympathy from everywhere – stokers, newspapers editors, the blacks at the settlement – all want to do something for his memory. And without him- the very spirit of the sunny isle – all things seem dreary."*[30]

In his book written in 1921, "The Last Leaves from Dunk Island", Dr Banfield includes a detailed description of the 1918 cyclone and its aftermath.

The following are several extracts taken from that publication.

He gives witness to the absolute fury of the cyclone. This is his culmination of those passages on *Page 9 Chapter One*.:

- *"Being in perfect sympathy with each other's fury, wind, rain and sea, in a common tongue, spoke threats of ruin and devastation, and fulfilled them all in more or less degree. And it has to be confessed that the crash and confusion of the awe-inspiring night, after three years of healing, still ring in the ears."*

On Page 10 Chapter Two, he continues:

- *"having thus disposed of the formalities of a great occasion, the pages to follow will be devoted to review of its consequences, not to human beings – and they are sad and disastrous enough – but to the natural features of the island, as they came to be revealed.*

    At sunrise on Sunday a leafy wilderness; at sunrise on Monday a leafless wilderness, wanting only grey skies, snow on the hills, and ice on the pools to suggest an English winter scene.

---

[30] Barbara Ross, "Different Leaves from Dunk Island", The Banfields, Dorothy Cottrell and the Singing Gold

Along the beach, on the flat, on the spurs of the range, astonishing transfiguration. The shrub-embroidered strand is now forlorn, its vegetation, uprooted and down beaten, naked roots exposed to critical view. Not a shrub has escaped, and broken and shattered limbs of tough trees appeal for sympathy. The country is foul with wreckage."

<u>On Page 12 Chapter Two</u>:

- *"Thousands of maritime birds were killed, and those of the land suffered in like degree. Here the only species which seems to be in pre-storm numbers is the swiftlet, the home of which, in secret places among huge granite rocks, was safe against the shake of anything less than an earthquake. Some shy birds have been made confiding by the stress of hunger. This is specially noticeable among the fruit-eating pigeons, which frequent the jungles. For several days these beautiful birds swarmed about <u>the ruins of the aboriginal settlement</u> on the mainland opposite, perching in protected spots at dark after a great deal of preliminary fluttering. This voluntary faith in the goodwill of man on the part of a timorous bird shows that the storm had destroyed its supplies and shelter."*

The Banfields at home taken not long after the cyclone on 1918 (note the stripped trees in the background.)

In 2011, Dunk Island was once again the victim of a ferocious cyclone, this time, Yasi.

I travelled through the Cassowary Coast several months after Yasi had reeked its havoc.

Dr Banfield's vivid descriptions of the destruction caused by the 1918 monster, mirrored what I witnessed there months after the actual dreadful event.

Chapter 11
Palm Island

Palm Island is located 65km north of Townsville in Cleveland Bay.

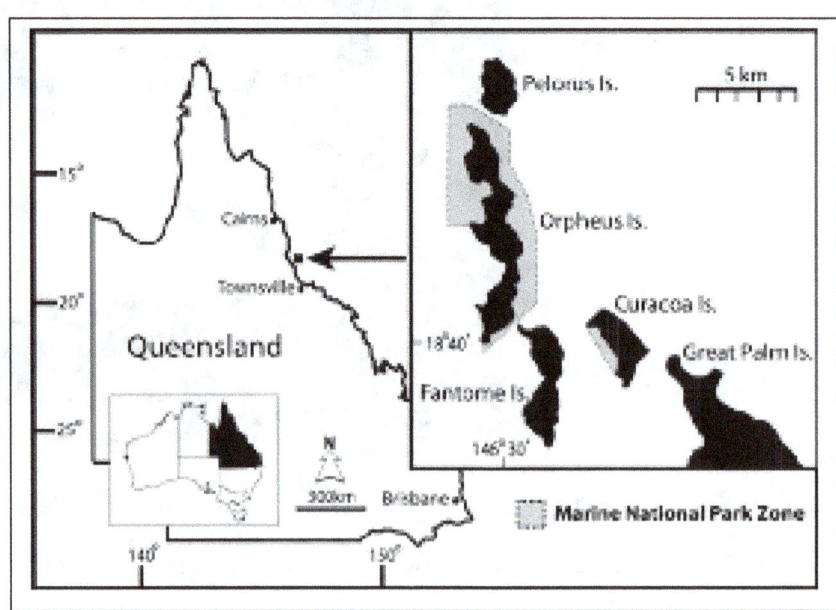

The original inhabitants of the island are thought to be the Manburra people (pronounced Munburra) though to this date, this has not been officially acknowledged by the Federal Court.

Palm Islanders kidnapped in 1883

In 1883, nine Palm Islanders were kidnapped by United States circus agent R. Cunningham and taken to the United States to become travelling exhibits in the Barnum and Bailey Circus. Most died obscure deaths overseas.

One of the men kidnapped from Palm Island was known as Kukamunburra (or) Tambo) and in 1993, his mummified body was found in the basement of a funeral parlour in Cleveland, Ohio. In 1994, Kukamunburra's body was repatriated from the United States and laid to rest on Palm Island in full ceremonial rites.[31]

---

[31] *Penelope Layland, Captive Lives, Moving Stories, (National Library of Australia news, Australia: 1998).*

The first record of the island was made by *Captain James Cook* when he named the Palm Island group during his exploration of the east coast of Australia. [32] Often called Greater Palm Island it is the largest of 16 islands within the group.

In 1819, *Captain Phillip Parker King* surveyed the east coast of Australia[33]. During his survey of Cleveland Bay he landed on one of the islands and recorded that:

"Near our landing-place were some natives' huts and two canoes; the former appeared to have been recently occupied, and were very snug habitations. They were of circular shape, and very ingeniously constructed by twigs stuck in the ground and arched over, the ends being artfully entwined so as to give support to each other; the whole was covered with a thatch of dried grass and reeds."

With the passing of the "Protection Act" which gave license to the government to take responsibility for the "welfare" of the Aboriginal population of Australia, sites were sought to which Aboriginal people may be "removed" from mainstream society for their "protection".

People removed were exiled from their cultural land and kinfolk, many never to again embrace the life left behind.

Palm Island had been considered suitable for this since it was first put forward in 1889 but was not gazetted until 1914 on recommendation of the first *Chief Protector Dr Walter Roth* who had visited the island in 1912.

The cyclonic destruction of the settlement at Hull River had left the residents virtually destitute. It was decided that rather than rebuild there, the whole settlement would be moved to Palm Island. All the building materials that could be salvaged were transported to Palm Island to be used there. By June 1918, the entire Hull River settlement had been relocated to Palm Island.

Returned Serviceman, *Robert Henry Curry* was installed as the first superintendent of the reserve.

Robert Henry Curry

1885-1930

---

[32] *James Cook and Sir William James Lloyd, Captain Cook's Journal during his first voyage round the world made in H.M. Bark 'Endeavour' 1768-71 (E Stock, United Kingdom)*
[33] *Captain Phillip Parker King, Narrative of a Survey of the intertropical and /western coasts of Australia performed between the years 1818 and 1822, Vol1 (John Murray, Australia: 1826), ch.5 at p197*

"Curry, utilising his military training, took regimental control supervising the residents in the clearing of the land and the construction of housing, having himself ensconced in a tent on the beach. Although criticised for his strict disciplinarian approach, he soon had the reserve up and running, albeit under Spartan conditions.

More than forty different language groups eventually arrived. Efforts were made to congregate like people together and locating them in areas to mirror their positions on the mainland.

A system of authoritarian apartheid was established.

White residents, school teacher, storekeepers and other staff were housed in "the white" section, in homes built by the Aboriginal residents.

Following construction of Mango Avenue by the Hull River people, it was subsequently declared "out of bounds" to all who were not white, with a gate barring access at each end of the road. Apartheid-like arrangement of space and design extended to the schools, with a "White school" for the children of officials and a "Native School" on opposite sides of the road. Children were separated from parents, and women from men, by confinement to dormitories."[34]

Mango Avenue Palm Island

ca. 1930

Superintendent Curry continued to strictly administer the reserve and in doing so, meted out harsh penalties – lengthy imprisonments, public humiliations, even floggings - to those who might threaten his control.

---

[34] *Joanne Watson, Palm Island – Through a long lens, Canberra, Aboriginal Studies Press. 2010*

After twelve years of the stress of maintaining such strict discipline on the island his mental well-being began to suffer. The loss of his wife in childbirth, finally tipped him over the edge. In the early hours of 3rd February 1930, Curry shot two people and burnt down the staff buildings including his own house, killing his son and step-daughter. He was later fatally shot by Peter Prior, an Aboriginal man who acted under instructions from Assistant Superintendent Thomas Hoffman.

"After an investigation into the shooting, Peter Prior and Thomas Hoffman were charged with Curry's murder. Peter Prior spent several months in jail before the case was heard by the Townsville Supreme Court. On14th August 1930. Justice R. J. Douglas concluded that the case should have never been brought to trial as the men's actions were justified, given the danger Curry posed to the community. The prosecution then decided to drop proceedings against the two men."[35]

Photographs relating to the Curry incident:[36]

Picture taken from the spot on the beach where Curry fell mortally wounded. The shot was fired from the window on the left of the picture

Inside the little schoolhouse where the court was held held.

My mother would have been seven years old if she had arrived on Palm Island with all the other Hull River refugees in 1918. I say refugees because that is exactly what they were – homeless and seeking shelter, driven by need from their cyclone decimated homes.

But what beheld them as they stepped ashore was not a scene of comfort and relief but one that meant even further hardship and desolation. Here they would endure the strict regime of Curry,

---

[35] *Australian Dictionary of Biography entry for Robert Curry; Sydney Morning Herald, 15 August 1930,p.11<hhtps://trove,nla.gov.au/newspaper/article 16665179*
[36] *Curry article Trove. Truth. Sunday .March 9 1930.(Trove.nla.gov.au) nla.news- page 22*

Superintendent of Palm Island, striving to clear the wilderness and build, not a place of their own, but a place in which they were to be incarcerated.

The saving grace of all this was that it took place on one of the most idyllic islands in the world. So amidst all the mayhem, much pleasure could be found in the pristine surroundings and as time went by and things more settled, this may have become even more the case. But it was a bitter pill for despite the beautiful natural environment, much hardship continued.

Survivors of the Hull River Cyclone 1918

I have endeavoured to present this story objectively but, in writing this, especially considering it is my own mother, grandmother and aunts who were actually enduring these conditions, it is difficult not to express outrage and shame at the treatment meted out by the government authorities at the time who sought to suppress the lives and culture of an entire race of human beings.

Here I'll take a step back one year to 1917 at the Hull River Settlement. Samuel Myquick passed away 29th September. His brother Nomoa on Badu Island had been notified of Sam's death by the Badu Island schoolteacher. Nomoa writes via the school teacher to request that Sam's wife and children be sent to Badu and placed in his care.

This correspondence took place between July and August 1918 and involved the Superintendent at Palm Thursday, requesting that Tibby and her two children be sent to Badu Island.

MYQUICK_MAIQUICK

Deaths, Reporting death of Samuel Myquick at Innisfail on 10/9/17 from Heart Failure following Pneumonia.

teacher at Badu has been advised of Samuel Myquick's death.

Misc, Nomoa wishes his sister-in-law Mrs Maiquick and two children to join him at Badu, S.T. [school teacher?] has no

Misc, Nomoa is unable to pay Mrs Maiquick's fare to Badu, but her two sons at Badu will assist her.

Misc, Tibbie Maiquick wishes to go to Badu. She came from Cooktown and was married at Yarrabah.

- *Reporting death of Samuel at Innisfail on 10/9/17 from Heart Failure following Pneumonia*
- *P.A. Thursday Island. The teacher at Badu Island has been advised of Samuel Myquick's death*
- *P.A. Thursday Island. Nomoa wishes his sister-in-law Mrs Maiquick and two children to join him at Badu, S.T. (school teacher) has no objection*
- *P.A. Thursday Island. Noama is unable to pay Mrs Maiquick's fare to Badu but her two sons at Badu will assist her. (The sons were Sam's now grown up children from his first wife).*
- *Superintendent Palm Island. Tibbie Maiquick wishes to go the Badu. She came from Cooktown and was married at Yarrabah.*

There is no record of Tibby's ever visiting Badu Island and it's odd that the request mentions only two children she had three children and perhaps another on the way.

Because of the recorded birth of her fourth child, a son, Samuel, I'm faced with the question of whether Tibby actually made it to Badu or if she went directly to Palm Island with the others in 1918.

Young 'Sammy' Myquick is reported to have been born in 1918 at Mapoon.[37] I cannot explain this because I know for certain that my mother was at the Hull River settlement during the cyclone in

---

[37] *Anna Shnukal genealogy for the Myquick family, Queensland death certificate for Sammy Myquick no.1935/C4780*

March 1918. I am also aware that young Sammy grew up on the "West Coast" (of Cape York) and tragically died at age 17 while working on a pearling lugger in Torres Strait. It is also reported that Tibby moved to Mapoon from Palm Island sometime after 1920 and all her subsequent children were born at or on the way to, Mapoon. That Sammy could have been born at Mapoon in 1918, is improbable.

Most likely, in June 1918, Tibby and the girls would have found themselves herded to Palm Island with the rest of the unfortunates.

The following report was published in The Mail, Adelaide, South Australia on 5th December 1935:[38]

- *"Brisbane, Saturday. When the pearling lugger 'Alidinia' reached Thursday Island today she had on board two dead men. They were Japanese diver, Ichitaro Miyao, 35, and a Mapoon Native, Sammy Myquick, 17. The lugger was working at Warrior Island with the diver down five fathoms. When no signals had been received for some time the captain went down and found Miyao dead in his diving dress. As the lugger was returning to Thursday Island Myquick was found dead in the hold. "The Government officer at the island found that the diver had died from heart failure, while the aborigine had been poisoned by fumes from a broken exhaust pipe in the engine."* (Some believe he really died from the bends in going to the rescue of Miyao.)

Pearling lugger "Alidinia" Torres Strait ca.1935[39]

Nomoa asked that Sam's widow and two children be sent to Badu. This could be taken to mean just Maria and Elizabeth were the children - excluding Gladys.

The exclusion here of Gladys is another instance of her being detached from her mother and siblings. I suspect that attention was given to her fairness from a very young age. I have already mentioned the comment made in the Hull River records that she was <u>"the only quadroon child on the settlement. Her parents wish to keep her but she would be better away."</u>

Further along, in a 1927 Report of the Palm Island Native School by Undersecretary McKenna, he describes her as <u>"a girl of European features and colour"</u>.

---

[38] <u>https://longstreath.com/community/incidents/?sortby=cod_6&sortdirection=desc&page=9</u>
[39] File:StateLibQld_1_76236Alidinia(Ship)jpg_Wikimedia Commons

I've been told that is common knowledge among our present day relatives that Gladys had been forbidden to mix with her family on Palm Island.

In 1920 Tibby married Johnny Mapoon on Palm Island. Johnny was born at Mapoon Mission in 1891. His parents were named Daniel and Marie.[40]

As far as can be ascertained Gladys remained on Palm Island from June 1918 to November 1927.

The following are extracts from the Auditors Report on the Books and Accounts for the Home Secretary's Office, Queensland showing wages earned by Gladys Myquick:[41]

6th April 1925 - 23rd May 1926

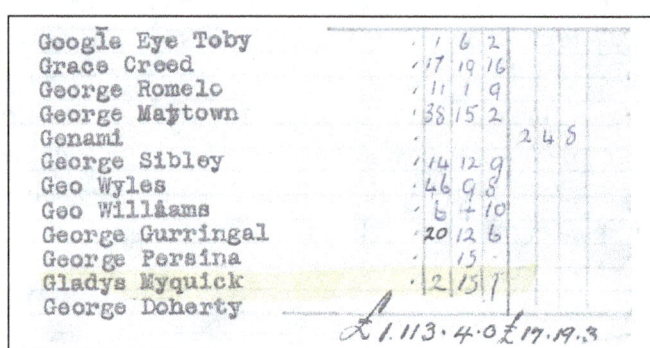

Gladys Myquick 2.15.7 (two pounds, fifteen shillings and seven pence)

23rd May 1927 – 2nd May 1928

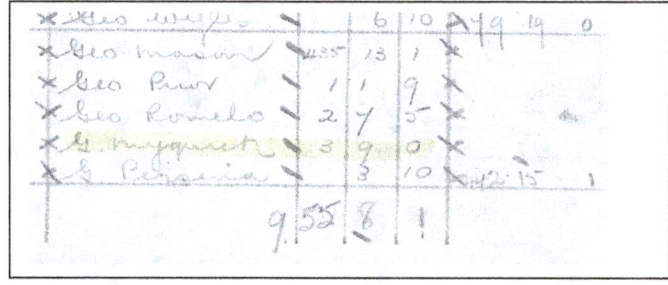

Gladys Myquick 3.9.0 (three pounds and nine shillings)

Below are copies of the original covering pages of each of the Reports that were made available for my research. The year 1926 – 1927 is not shown but it may be assumed that wages were earned during that year also.

---

[40] *Departmental identification card for Johnny Mapoon.*
[41] *Chief Auditor's Report on the books and Accounts of the Aboriginal Settlement at Palm Island 1926-28*

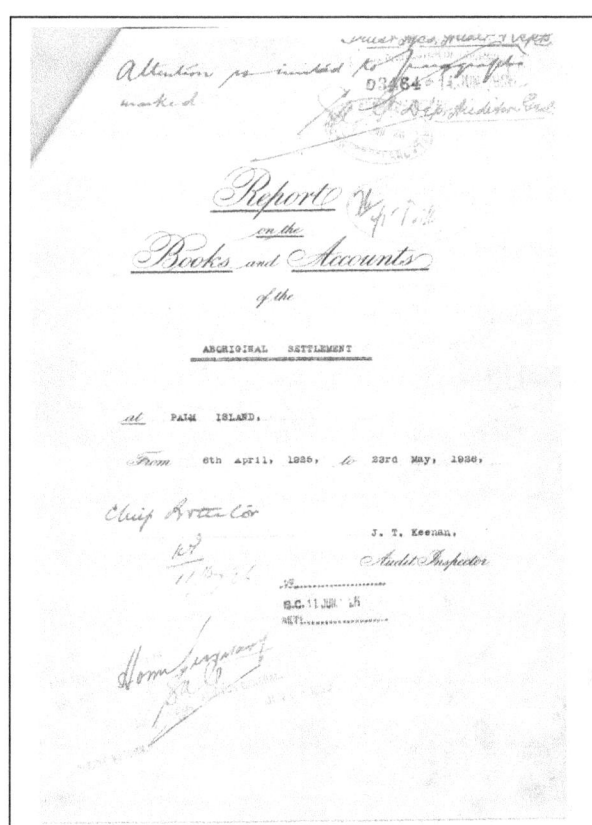
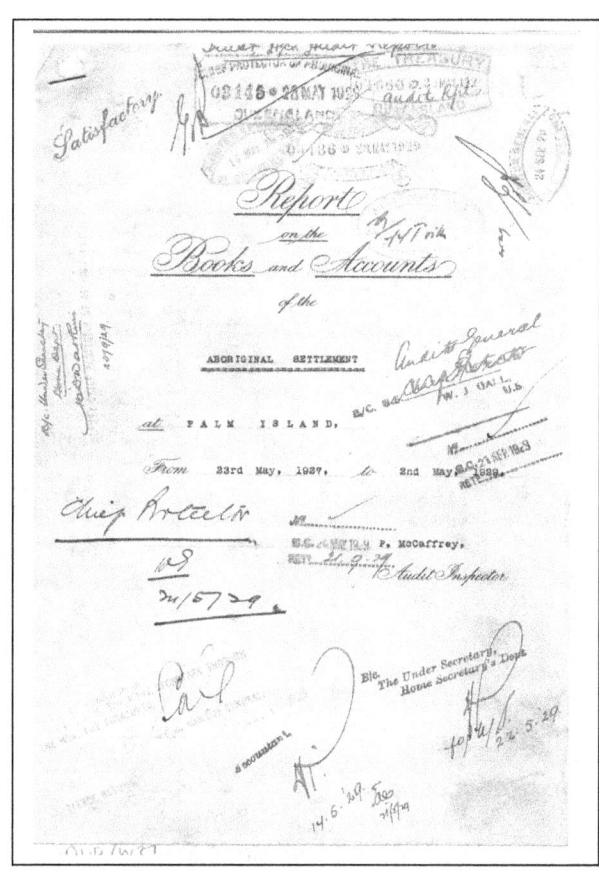

The wages earned were in her occupation as a teacher's assistant at the Palm Island Native School during the years 1925 to 1927 when she was fourteen to sixteen years of age.

Below is a copy of the original Report on the Native School at Palm Island by Undersecretary McKenna for the Department of Public Instruction Brisbane on the 4th of June 1927.[42]

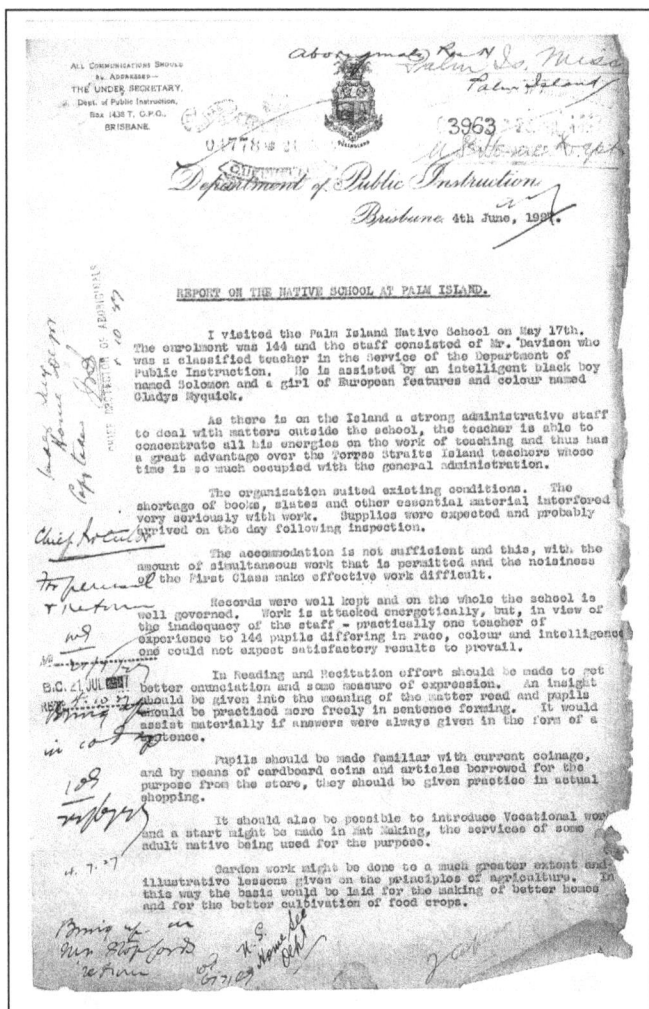

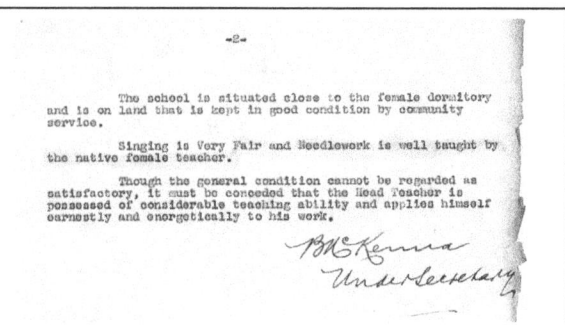

The report reads:

- "I visited the Palm Island School on May 17th. The enrolment was 144 and the staff consisted of Mr. Davison who was a classified teacher in the service of the Department of Public Instruction. He is assisted by an intelligent black boy named Solomon and a girl of European features and colour named Gladys Myquick.

    As there is on the Island a strong administrative staff to deal with matters outside school, the teacher is able to concentrate all his energies on the work of teaching and thus has a great advantage over Torres Strait Island teachers whose time is so much occupied with general administration.

    The organisation suited existing conditions. The shortage of books, slates and other essential materials interfered very seriously with work. Supplies were expected and probably arrived on the day following inspection.

---

[42] HOM/ J635,27/4778, Report on the Native School at Palm Island by ndersecretaryB.McKenna1927

The accommodation is not sufficient and this, with the amount of simultaneous work that is permitted and the noisiness of the First class make effective work difficult.

Records were well kept and on the whole the school is well governed. Work is attacked energetically, but in view of the inadequacy of the staff – practically one teacher of experience to 144 pupils differing in race, colour and intelligence, one could not expect satisfactory results to prevail.

In Reading and Recitation effort should be made to get better enunciation and some measure of expression. An insight should be given into the meaning of the matter read and pupils should be practised more freely in sentence forming. It would assist materially if answers were always given in the form of a sentence.

Pupils should be made familiar with current coinage, and by means of cardboard coins and articles borrowed for this purpose from the store, they should be given practice in actual shopping.

It should also be possible to introduce Vocational work and a start might be made in Mat Making, the services of some adult native being used for the purpose.

Garden work might be done to a much greater extent and illustrative lessons given on the principles of agriculture. In this way the basis would be laid for the making of better homes and for the better cultivation of food crops.

The school is situated close to the female dormitory and is on land that is kept in good condition by community service.

Singing is Very Fair and <u>Needlework is well taught by the native female teacher.</u>

Though the general condition cannot be regarded as satisfactory, it must be conceded that the Head Teacher is possessed of considerable teaching ability and applies himself earnestly and energetically to his work.

B.McKenna

Undersecretary"

The report certainly gives good insight into the situation at the Palm Island Native School in 1927.

McKenna makes mention of Gladys in two instances, once as "a girl of European features and colour" and second, as needlework instructor.

As an adult, Gladys was known for her fine needlework and other craftwork. She would post mail-orders for patterns and iron-on transfer designs to be used for embroidery on table linen and other purposes. Her hands were dexterous and rarely idle.

By 1927, Tibby had borne six children, Gladys, Maria, Elizabeth, Samuel, Lottie and Doris.

On the 8th November of that year, the family was being transported from Palm Island to Thursday Island on the "S.S. Kallatina" when approaching Cairns, Tibby gave birth on board to her seventh child.

Of course, the birth caused quite a stir aboard the ship and even more so when the story was relayed to shore and the local press got wind of the event and submitted the article below:[43]

"Birth at Sea

While the John Burke steamer Kallatina was in the vicinity of Green Island just outside Cairns about 10.45 o'clock yesterday morning, the wife of Johnny Mapoon, a Murray Island native who was one of the deck passengers on their way to Thursday Island, gave birth to a baby girl. The mother was attended by Mrs. Saki, another Murray Islander. It is intended to call the child Kathleen Kallatina Burke Mapoon. She is a fine healthy baby. On the Kallatina's arrival in Cairns, the agents for the vessel Messrs. Samuel Allen and Sons Ltd. got in touch with the police who arranged for the government medical officer to see the mother and child. Both were found to be doing well, and permission was given for them to proceed. While the Kallatina was in port, about 50 of the parents' country people visited the boat, expressing their congratulations on the birth of a daughter lucky enough to bear the same name of a ship and its owner. The smoke room of the vessel had been placed at the disposal of the mother and child, and the master, Captain Masterman, started a subscription list from which it is hoped to be able to present the parents with 10 (pounds)"

---

[43] *Cairns Post Qld(1909-1945 9Nov1927*

S S Kallatina docked on Clarence River Grafton ca. 1900

- *"**KALLATINA** 646 gross tons, 380 net. Lbd: 179'1"x28'2"x11'4". Steel steamship built by D J Dunlop Co., Port Glasgow, 1890. Built as a passenger vessel for the Clarence, Richmond & Macleay River S N Co registerd Sydney. The only new addition to the Company under this title. September 1891 of this concern working the north coast run. Sold to John Burke Ltd., Brisbane in June of 1921 and altered to measure 628 gross tons and 306 net. J Burke employed her on the Queensland coastal run and taking in the Gulf of Carpentaria ports until sold circa 1930 and hulked in 1931; lying as a breakwater on Moreton Island, off Tangalooma."[44]*

So the family proceeded to Thursday Island and eventually on to the Mapoon Mission on the west coast of Cape York.

---

[44] *http://www.flotilla-australia.com.crrsnco.htm12/04/2009*

Chapter 12
Mapoon Mission

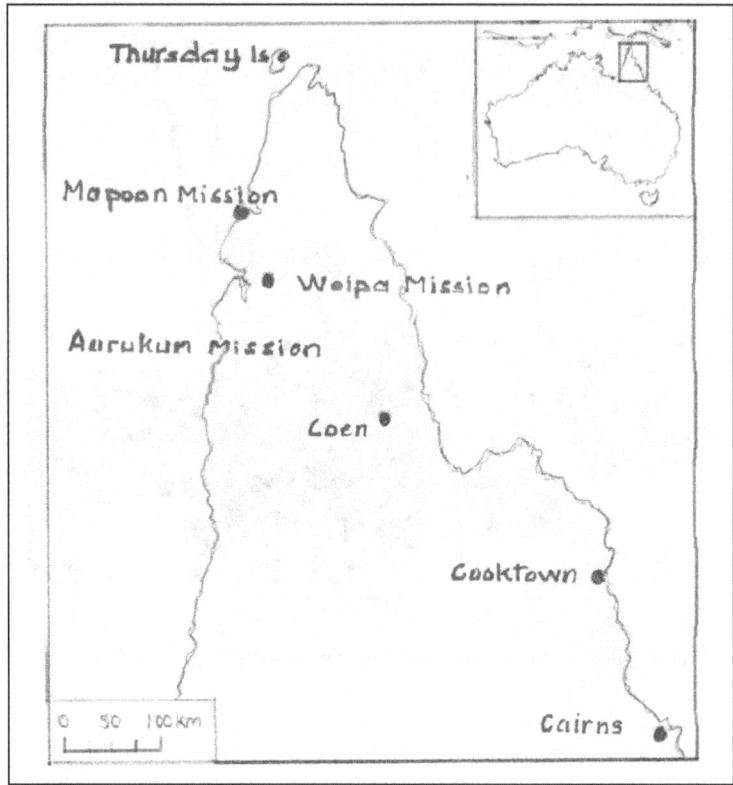

Mapoon, a small village and a former Aboriginal reserve, is on the west coast of Cape York Peninsula, near the entrance to Port Musgrave. It is 75km north of Weipa and 170 km south-west of the tip of the peninsula.

In 1891 the Government Resident at Thursday Island proposed the establishment of a chain of missions for the 'protection' of Aborigines being displaced by the spread of European pastoralism. The Presbyterian Church supported the proposal and engaged Moravian missionaries who had been active in the mission field for decades. Cullen Point on Port Musgrave was chosen and named Mapoon Mission. It is thought that the name was an Aboriginal expression describing the sandy beach inside the entrance to Port Musgrave. Houses, a school and a church were erected. The mission was described in the Australian Handbook, including remarks on the 'civilising' ideology underpinning the enterprise.

In 1899 it was estimated that the mission had 400 inhabitants. In 1908, Mapoon was designated an industrial School (for taking children forcibly removed from their families). The reserve then included an extensive area from north of Mapoon to south of the Archer River (Aurukun). At this time, there were an estimated 1500 Aborigines on the reserve.

In addition to fruit and vegetable crops, a cattle herd was kept and numbered 100 head in the 1930s. Soon after World War II a geological investigation confirmed the presence of good quality bauxite deposits. Large prospecting leases were taken out in 1957 when an Act of Queensland Parliament assigned 5780 sq km of Reserve land on medium and long term (100 year) leases to Comalco. An

Alcan mining lease assigned 1388 sq km in 1965. The mission closed in 1962 in anticipation of the removal of the Mapoon population to enable mining to proceed. The community resisted, and evictions and building demolition followed in1963.

Some inhabitants went to New Mapoon, near Bamaga at the top of Cape York, and the last of those evicted were sent to Weipa. In 1974 several former Mapoon families returned to Old Mapoon, aided by a Commonwealth grant. The settlement was officially returned to the Aboriginal people in 1989. In 2002 Mapoon Aboriginal Council was created, administering an area of 530 sq km.[45]

The name "Mapoon" described its sandy beaches.

The mission was established as an industrial school in 1916.

---

[45] *J. Roberts et al, eds, The Mapoon Story, 3 volumes, Fitzroy, Vic, International Development Action, 1975*

It may be assumed that Gladys made the journey to Mapoon on board the Kallatina with the rest of the family. It has been said by people who knew her later on Thursday Island that she had arrived there from Mapoon.

The following extract from the correspondence of Superintendent Robert Curry at Palm Island seeking audience with the Chief Protector Bleakley seems to confirm this also. It is most likely addressed to Cornelius O'Leary who was aboriginal protector for the district of Somerset as this places the correspondence to have occurred sometime between 1927 and 1929. (A/8725 is the Archive number for the document)

- The first issue involves concern for the well-being of the mission people:

"*No.9. I also ask you to force the chief Protector to inspect the Mission Stations where they are starving. I can quote Mona Mona *and the Superintendent told me he owed so much for stores he was forced to turn the natives bush until he could pay. *(Mona Mona was a Seventhday Adventist Mission established near Kuranda.)*

Mapoon Mission I have letters from the Myquick family that they want to come back as they only got cocoa nuts to eat for dinner.

I'm supposing that one of the older children, probably Gladys who was a teenager by this time, wrote the letter of complaint and signed with her name 'Myquick' as Tibby and the younger children would have had the name 'Mapoon' by then.

- The second issue involves Ernest Gribble:

"Yarrabah turned a man named Gribble out as he was not wanted by them, but I see Mr. Bleakley is getting this man to come to Palm Island to teach the natives hiddoctrine that they rejected on Yarrabah."

- The reply came from O'Leary:

"The reference to Gribble is of no concern of mine, any reference to his conduct would be better answered by authorities of the Anglican Church, who are asking that he be appointed Chaplain and reside on Palm Island."

Ernest Gribble was chaplain to Palm Island settlement from 1929 to 1931 after a long stint in Western Australia following his breakdown at Yarrabah in 1910.

Johnny Mapoon, Tibby and the children remained at Mapoon until 1939 when they returned to Palm Island. Tibby's eighth child, Iris was born at Mapoon. Her son Sammy passed away on Thursday Island in 1935. Tibby named her ninth child born in 1939, Samuel also in his memory. Sadly this Samuel lived just a few short months.

Gladys did not remain at Mapoon with the family. It has been said that friction occurred between Gladys and one of her sisters. This seems to be the catalyst that prompted Gladys to leave Mapoon and to sail to Thursday Island. The story also goes that her sister was so upset at Gladys's leaving that she waded out into the ocean following the boat taking her away begging her to stay.

They say they never saw Gladys again after that day.

There is much evidence in the documents to suggest that Gladys was often made to feel that she was out of place in the environments where she grew up.

It is only natural for her to want to find her own place in the world.

Her escape from the settlement was the beginning of a new life for her. She found gainful employment on the island and enjoyed a happy social life.

It was there that she was made aware of the possibility of shedding the shackles of her past life and of grasping an opportunity to become a citizen of mainstream Australia, something that in all her young life as an Indigenous person, had been denied to her.

When offered the key to the prison it's no surprise when it's accepted!

The view of Torres Strait taken from a hill on Thursday Island

during my visit there in 2011.

Chapter 13
Cooktown

Cooktown ca. 1910

The Cooktown area plays such an important role in my mother's beginnings that I think a look at its history is most appropriate. I have already touched on this in my chapter on my great grandmother, Maggie and our Guugu Yimithirr people but I will now expand a little on that.

The site of modern Cooktown was the meeting place of two vastly different cultures, when in June, 1770, the local Guugu Yimithirr watched the crippled Endeavour make its way into the mouth of their' Wahalumbal' river and saw Europeans for the first time.

Cook wrote in his journal:

- "it was happy for us that a place of refuge was at hand."[46]

The crew spent seven weeks repairing the ship, refurbishing supplies and caring for their sick. Local plant specimens were collected by botanist Joseph Banks and naturalist Daniel Solander and many were illustrated by young artist, Sydney Parkinson.

The first recorded sightings of kangaroos by Europeans was on Grassy Hill, which rises above the place where the ship was beached. Cook climbed this hill to work out a safe passage for the Endeavour to sail through the surrounding reefs after it was repaired.

"The visit ended on 19th July 1770 in a skirmish after Cook refused to share turtles he had kept on board with the locals. They set fire to the grass around Cook's camp twice, burning the area and

---

[46] *From Cook's Journal Archived*

killing a suckling pig. After Cook wounded one of the men with a musket, they ran away. Cook, Banks and some others followed them and caught up with them on a rocky bar near Furneaux Street, which is now known as Reconciliation Rocks. A "little old man" appeared from the pursued group and the parties were reconciled. This is an important historic event as it is believed that this is the first recorded reconciliation between Europeans and Indigenous Australians ever."[47]

Cook named the river "Endeavour" after his ship, and as they sailed north, he hoisted the flag known as the "Queen Anne Jack" and claimed possession of the whole eastern coast of Australia for Britain. He named Cape York Peninsula after the then Duke of York and Albany ("The Grand Old Duke of York")

The next recorded European expedition to the area was nearly 50 years later, when botanist, Alan Cunningham, accompanying Captain Phillip Parker King, visited the region in 1819-20. King also named the mountain which forms a backdrop to Cooktown, Mt Cook.

"Natives of Endeavour River in a canoe, fishing." From Phillip Parker King's Survey. 1818.

"Manner in which Natives of the East Coast strike turtle." From Phillip Parker King's Survey. 1818.

Cooktown is now one of the few large towns in Cape York Peninsula and was founded on 25th October 1873 as a supply port for the goldfields along the Palmer River. It was called "Cook's Town" until 1st June 1874.

Gold had been discovered in the Palmer River area, to the south west. The gold rush brought prospectors from all over the world which led to rapid expansion of the town.

The Chinese who flocked to the area played an important role in the early days of Cooktown. Although originally here for the gold, many established market gardens and other commercial outlets.

In 1881, a bridge over the Endeavour River was completed which opened up the rich pastoral lands of the Endeavour and McIvor River area. (Sonata has been referred to as a "selection". It is probable that the Gortons took up this selection at McIvor around this time. William was reported to have

---

[47] *"James Cook, the Endeavour River, Cooktown", Australian National Trust*

been playing cricket in Cooktown in 1880. He may even had been the postmaster before taking up the selection).

In 1886 the Lutheran church established several missions in the area to create a secure place for the Aboriginal people living in abominable conditions on the edge of town. Missions were built at Elim, Wyal, and Bloomfield.

Also in 1888, five Irish nuns from the Sisters of Mercy order arrived in Cooktown and established a Convent School. (The original building is now used as the James Cook Museum).

The James Cook Museum (previously the Convent School)

The photo was taken on my visit to Cooktown in 2011

With the gold rush over, the number of people living in the area began to dwindle. Two major fires struck Cooktown in 1875 and again in 1919 when whole blocks of buildings in the main street were burned to the ground. A major cyclone in 1907 added further destruction.

Mary Watson

This is one of the many stories told by my mother. The story goes down as part of North Queensland's folklore. I will just deliver a short synopsis of it here.

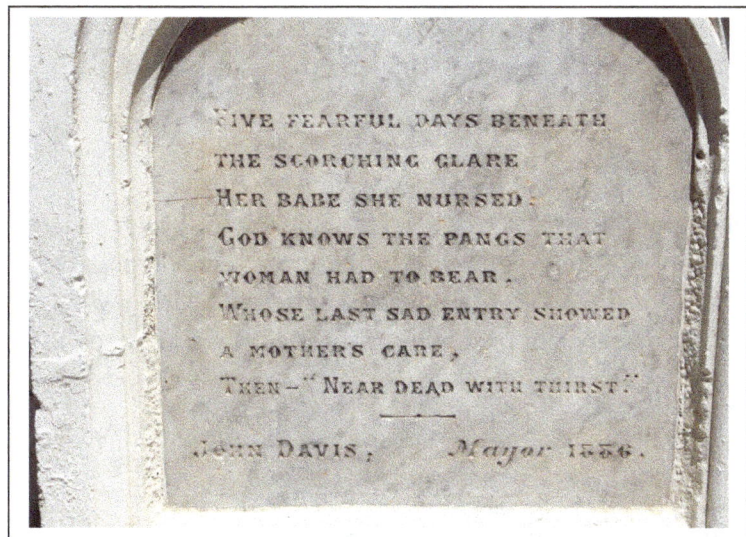

The inscription reads:

Five fearful days beneath

The scorching glare

God knows the pangs

That woman had to bear,

Whose last sad entry showed

A mother's care,

Then – "Near dead with thirst"

John Davis   Mayor 1886

Monument to the Mary Watson tragedy Cooktown

Mary Watson, her infant son and Chinese servant Ah Sam escaped an attack by local Aboriginal people at Lizard Island in 1881 by rowing away in an iron beche-de-mere tank. The small group survived eight days at sea before succumbing to dehydration. Mrs Watson had left her diary behind in her hut but maintained a makeshift diary up to the day of her death. It, along with her bible was discovered with her body. Both diaries are held in the John Oxley Library and her bible is in the Queensland Museum. [48]

The beche-mere tank in which Mary Watson, her son and Ah Sum made their escape

---

[48] *Queensland Historical Atlas, Histories, Cultures, Landscapes*

Chapter 14
The Gortons

William Vernon Leathes Gorton was born in Sydney in 1853. His parents were Charles Frederick Gorton (b.1806) and Emily Duncombe (b.1821) from Dorschester, Dorset, England.

He married Marion Chapman on 22 May 1878. Marion was the daughter of David Winter Chapman and Mary Ann Wright. She was born in 1821 in London, England

In the mid-1800s, they took up a pastoral property in the McIvor River area near Cooktown and named it "Sonata". All my endeavours to locate precisely where this property was actually situated have been in vain. I suspect it may have been absorbed into the Hopevale Lutheran Mission when it was established in 1949. I can find no records of change of ownership but the Gortons departed the area sometime during or before the 1920s.

Between the years 1879 to 1893 William and Marion had eight children – Frederick, Marion, Vernon, Newman, William, Ruby, Glen and Monte.

An article in the Cairns Post in June 1910 mentioned William's attendance at the local Cooktown Show:

- *"At the showgrounds and racecourse some very well-known faces of the Cook District were to be seen, amongst whom may be mentioned Mr W Gorton of Sonata, McIvor…………"* [49].

Also in his early days at Cooktown:

- *"A cricket match, Bachelors versus Benedicts, was held at Savage's Two Mile, Cooktown on Saturday, September 18, 1880. The statement is made that as usual the Benedicts were beaten two to one Bachelors' team: Nicholas, Gannon, Stitt, C Wallace, Gordon, A Wallace, Scott, Cooper, Marrett and Jones. Total 102. A Wallace contributing 36 not out. Benedicts' team: Knight, Fitzgerald, Gorton, Olive, Forbes, Fahey, Carroll, Lawrence, Beardmore, Thompson, Standen. Total 53. Sundries 23 was highest scorer for the Benedicts."* [50]

Perhaps William Gorton was a better cattleman than a cricketer. Some of the names here can be linked to local properties, for example, Wallace, Olive. These names have also cropped up in my research of the area.

Little Ruby (aged about 8 years old) also made the newspaper in 1897 when she entered a contest run by (nom de plume) 'Dame Durden' in which children were encouraged to write letters to the newspaper and the best selected would receive a prize.

Ruby's reply to the letter informing her of her win:

- *"Dear Dame Durden,
Last Saturday week I was sitting in the room with mother, and the mail came and someone said, "There's a book for Ruby." We thought it was from our aunty in Brisbane, but when I opened it I saw it was from you, that was better still. Oh, I was pleased, and thank you so much dear Dame Durden. I have read such a lot of stories in it. I will take care of it, as it is a*

---

[49] *Cairns Post (Qld.: 1909-1954), Tuesday 21 June 1910. Page 3*
[50] *http://trove.nla.gov.au/newspaper/edition/nla.news- article 42145861.*

first prize I have ever got. Now, I will tell you about my toys. I have a set of cows and calves made out of wood, which my brothers made, I put them out in the rain, and the wood swells, so then I say they have been turned out to grass, as they really do get so fat.

I have a doll's house, made out of a tea chest, which Mamma made me and she lined it with a pretty bright material, and it has a little carpet floor. I have lots of doll's beds made out of greenhide. It is a new fashion, don't you think so?

Now, goodbye dear Dame Durden, with plenty of love, from your little friend.

Ruby Gorton"

Dame Durden:
You must tell me about this fashion. I like to know about doll's houses, and I have never heard of this kind of bed."[51]

In June 1898, Walter Roth spent some time in the McIvor River Area and further north to the Starcke River accompanying the Gold Warden, police and trackers on their inspection of conditions in the goldmining in the area.

In his role as ethnologist, he recorded what he was able to observe of the local indigenous languages. He reported that the 'blacks' around the Gorton's selection "Sonata" spoke 'par-ra". His report included the following observations:

- *"(a) These Starcke River blacks whom I visited at Munbarra speak Koko-yimidir (Guuguyimithirr), as at Cooktown, Cape Bedford, etc. Their walkabout includes Cooktown, camping at the 2 mile, the McIvor, Cape Bedford, and the mouth of the Starcke itself, where they meet the coast blacks, who speak koko-jom-bol, and koko-yim-bol.*
- *(b) The koko-jombol speaking aboriginals inhabit the coast line from the mouth of the Starcke R. round to Cape Flattery. They walk about down the coast to the mouth of the McIvor River where they meet the Cape Bedford and McIvor blacks and up the banks of the Starcke as far as Munbarra.*
- *© The koko-yimbol speaking blacks inhabit the coastline from the mouth of the Starcke as far certainly as Barrow Point, travelling a little way up both the Jeannie and Starcke Rivers.*

From the fact of the Munbarra (Starcke River) people being able to communicate with the koko-jom-bol and koko-yimbol speaking blacks, there cannot be much difference in their dialects and that of the Cooktown (koko-yimidir speaking) individuals.

At the time of my arrival at Munbarra, all the local aborigines, except two, fled down the river, and up into the mountains, at the sight of the police and trackers, These two, who had been brought into Cooktown last year for treatment for spear wounds by constable Waters, as soon as they recognized our peacable intentions, collected as far as they could all within reach, and by nightfall-fall there must have been quite a score collected at a spot about 200 yards from our camp. I gave the women and children numerous presents of beads, and Jew's harps and the men tobacco, and had a long talk with them all. They told me they bolted because they thought I was going to take them all away: needless to say I dispelled this illusion, and told them that so long as they did not steal from the digger's tents, or behave "saucy" to them nothing would be done to harm them. They all appeared very happy and contented with their lot, and well fed, and easily

---

[51] *http://trove.nla.gov.au/npd/del/article71293369   ;*

earn food by "dollying" for the miners – this work they speak of in pigeon-english as "Kill him stone".[52]

As Dr Roth spent much time in the area, it is probable that he mingled socially with the local land owners including the Gortons. Some evidence of this is in the recorded official correspondences which passed between them.

The Gorton's respect for the local Aboriginal people is illustrated in the following letter in which William Gorton writes to **Superintendent King** informing him of an incident involving a group of Aboriginal boys:[53]

    Sonata

19/3/05

Supt King
(Protector of Aboriginals Cooktown)
Dear Sir,
I think it's only right to bring under your notice and consideration the following good service rendered by the blacks of the McIvor to the late Isaac Coates during his illness. Coates was found ill and helpless in his hut by two (2) boys who got

him food and water, then went off for assistance (On Coates desire) to carry him into town. At 4pm on Thursday, they made a start and after going a few miles found they were unequal for the task. Some of them went for more assistance, and left the others to camp with Coates that night at the Cocoa Creek turn off road. They returned on Friday morning with more boys and carried him as far as Thygeson's Creek that day. The following ....

---

[52] *Col/139Microfilmz1604Frame No's 593-599*
[53] *A/58782,CR707,ItemID:336502*

day they carried him to Williams's Gate and got Williams to send his dray and take him on to Millers. At this place the boys all returned. There were seven (7) boys engaged in this task. They were all promised clothes, tobacco etc. by the late Mr Coates for their service when he returned. As Coates died soon after reaching town, and left a good big estate behind, I think these boys should receive from your hands, some recompense for this good service and kind action, and for the encouragement of anything of this kind in future. The estate can well afford to pay them. There six (6) boys from McIvor and one more from Thygeson's as below. We are all ready enough to bring under your notice the Blacks bad actions, so I think it only fair if we try to do their good ones. (Jackey, Johnny C, Toby coates, Toby Stuckey, Tumby, Harry, and Mill.. from Thygesons)

Yours, W L Gorton

- Sergeant King then forwards Gorton's letter to Dr Roth Chief Protector in Brisbane:

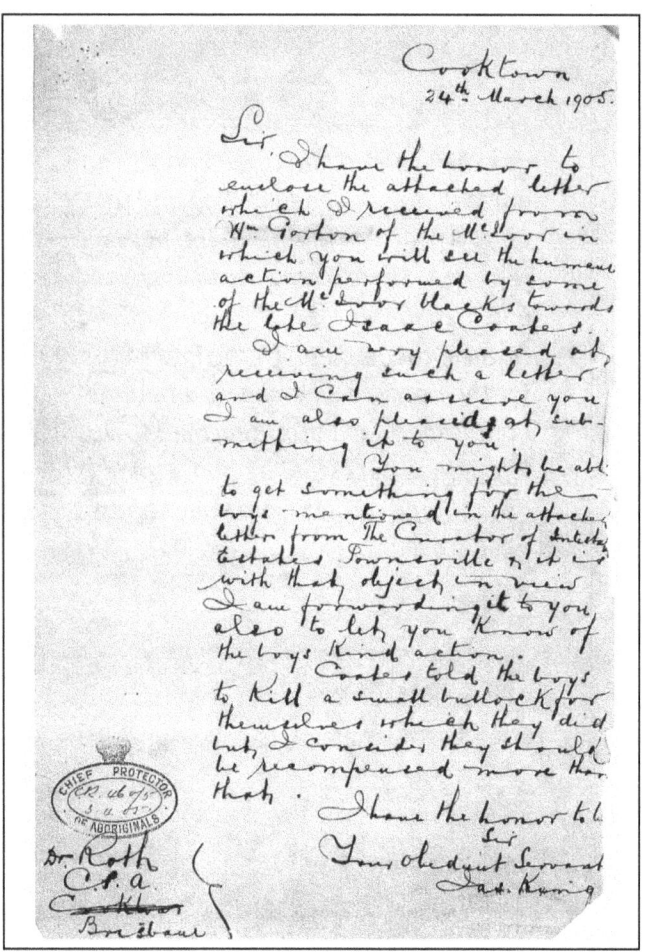

                              Cooktown 24th March 1905

- *Sir,*

I have the honour to enclose the attached letter which I received from Wm Gorton of the McIvor in which you will see the humane action performed by some of the McIvor blacks towards the late Isaac Coates.

You might get something for the boys from The Curator of Intestate Estates Townsville and it is with that object in view I am forwarding it to you also to let you know of the boys' kind action.

Coates told the boys to kill a small bullock for themselves which they did but consider they should be recompensed more than that.

I have the honour to be,

Sir, Your obedient Servant,

Chas King

- This reply came from the Office of Insolvency Intestacy and Insanity, Townsville.10th April 1905:

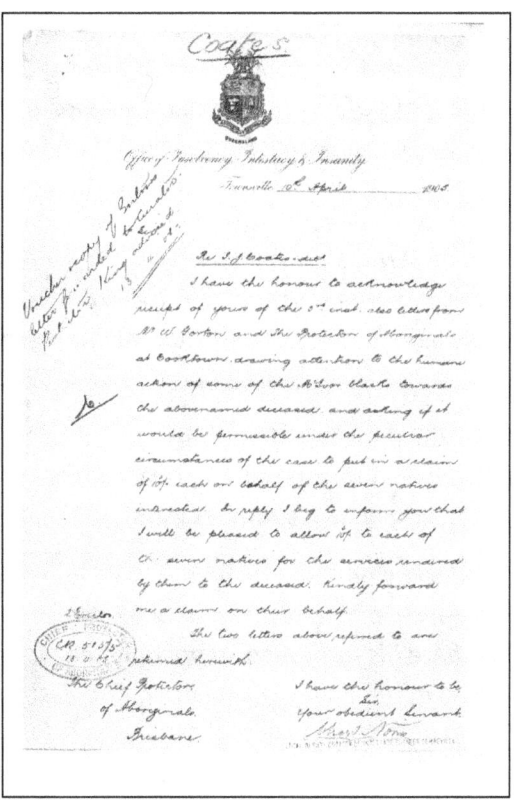

- Re. I.J.Coates –dec

I have the honour to acknowledge receipt of yours of the 3rd inst. Also letters from Mr W. Gorton and The Protector of Aboriginals at Cooktown drawing attention to the humane action some of the McIvor blacks towards the above-named deceased and asking if it would be permissible under the peculiar circumstances of the case to put in a claim of 10/- each on behalf of the seven natives interested. In reply I beg to inform you that I will be pleased to allow 10/- to each of the seven natives for the services rendered by them to the deceased. Kindly forward me a claim on their behalf.

The two letters above referred to are returned herewith.

I have the honour to be,	[voucher and copy of Gorton's
Sir,	letter forwarded to Curator
Your obedient Servant,	Protector King advised.13.4.05]

Chas S Norris (Local Deputy Curator of Intestates Townsville)

So the boys each received their 10/- (ten shillings) each thanks to the kind intervention of William Gorton who thought the boys deserving of reward for their struggles to assist the dying Mr Coates.

It is difficult to ascertain just when the Gorton family left the Cooktown district but William's obituary is recorded in Mackay in 1929.

- *"The death is announced of Mr. William Vernon Gorton, one of the North Queensland pioneers. For some 40 years Mr. Gorton lived in Cooktown in the McIvor River country in the earlier days of its development. He was a son of the late C.F. Gorton R.N. and a brother of Mrs. Hervey Fitzgerald of Clayfield and Miss Gorton of South Brisbane. He is survived by his widow, two daughters and five sons, who live at Marian, Mackay, at which centre he passed his later days. Mr. W. V. Gorton was a cultured man, and in the Cooktown district was very much respected. He did pioneering work, and was a courageous and unselfish colonist of the North in the days when settlement of the rich lands there often meant a great deal of hardship."[54]*

It seems that the family all moved to Mackay initially but perhaps spread further afield as time went by. The only other member of the family I have information on, is William's son Glen. A quite expansive obituary was written for him on Friday 13 November 1953:

- *"The death occurred in Mackay on Tuesday of a well-known and respected Bowen district pastoralist in Mr Glen Gorton, at the age of 62 years. The late Glen Gorton was born in Cooktown where his father was a postmaster. As a young man he managed Urapnah Station in the Collinsville district, and in the early 20s took up land at Bloomsbury. He was an able cattleman and made a specialty of taking up undeveloped country and improving it extensively. He did this with several properties in succession. After selling his Bloomsbury holding he took up the Oakdale holding on top of the Sarina Range, and disposed of this later to open up Glensfield, in the Blue Mountain district. His next holding was Lilypond near Prosperpine. He next owned a property at Koumain, and latterly a holding at Mount Convenient.*

  He was keenly interested in district shows, and loved a good horse. Other Bowenites will remember prize-winning hacks and jumpers shown by him, some of them ridden by the late "Teddy" Gordon. He is survived by his wife, Mrs Mary Elizabeth Gorton, who before her marriage was Matron Middleton of the Bowen Hospital, and two sons, Messrs. E.M. Gorton (St Lawrence), and V.G.M. Gorton (Cloncurry). Two brothers, Messrs F. Gorton (N.S.W.), and J. Gorton (Brisbane) and one sister, Mrs. W. Cameron (Mirani) also survive him. Another brother, William, predeceased him. The funeral took place in Mackay on Wednesday."

So while much can be found regarding the history of the Sonata Gortons, little can be revealed as to their time following their departure.

---

[54] *The Brisbane Courier (Qld: 1864-1933), Friday 31 May 1929, page 21*

The old Cooktown hospital now a local church

Was this tree by the Endeavour River living at the time of Cook's arrival ?

Black Mountain near Cooktown

Chapter 15

An Exemption

"Section 33 of the 1897 Act made provision for the Minister to issue any half-caste, who, in his opinion, ought not to be subject to the provisions of this Act, a certificate...that such a half-caste is exempt from the provisions of this Act....Certificates of exemption were sought by hundreds of Aboriginal people who wished to escape the oppressive conditions enforced upon them by the Act. In many cases the Aboriginal person wishing to become exempt would write or request the local Protector or anyone else to write on his or her behalf to the Chief Protector requesting exemption.

The request would often be accompanied by letters of reference which confirmed that the Aboriginal person seeking exemption was of good character and did not associate with other Aborigines.

These characteristics as well as the ability to manage one's own affairs were the basis on which exemptions were usually granted.

Exemption from the Act did not always ensure, however, that money and property would not remain under the control of the Chief Protector.

Exemptions could also be revoked at any time whereupon the person would again be subject to the conditions set dawn b the Act."[55]

By satisfying all the necessary criteria, Gladys Myquick was granted exemption which meant that she was given freedom but must remain apart from her family who did not seek exemption at that time. So by the conditions of exemption, she then entered into a life devoid of family comfort and support until she eventually began one of her own.

---

[55] *A Brief History of the Government Administration of Aboriginal and Torres Strait Islander Peoples in Queensland*

Unknown European

It was the discovery of the Yarrabah Baptism Records that had led me out of the fog of my ignorance. By this I was able to determine my mother's maternal line back as far as her mother, Tibby and her grandmother, Maggie and her grandfather, Robert Mc Andrew. But one cloud was yet to be lifted and that was the identity of the "Unknown European" who is listed as my mother's father.

It was at this stage, that I thought I had come to end of the road and should feel content with all I had found so far. But not one to give up easily, I decided to enlist the help of family tracer extraordinaire – "Ancestry.com". I volunteered a saliva sample and waited in hope of a good result.

When my results did come in, they confirmed all that I had learned through my own endeavours in that my roots began in England and Ireland (from my father's side), Scotland (from Robert McAndrew and Australia (from Maggie).

"Ancestry.com" uses the science of DNA (Deoxyribonucleic acid) to 'match' people with similar chromosome characteristics. Autosomal DNA testing is the method used for this.

"Autosomal DNA is contained in the 22 pairs of chromosomes not involved in determining a person's sex. Autosomal DNA recombines each generation and new offspring receive one set on chromosomes from each parent. These are inherited exactly equally from both parents and roughly equally from grandparents to about 3 x great-grand parents.[56] *Therefore, the number of markers inherited from a specific ancestor decreases by about half each generation: that is, an individual receives half of their markers from each parent, about a quarter of their markers from each grandparent; about an eighth of their markers from each great-grandparent etc. Inheritance is more random and unequal from more distant ancestors".*[57]

For several years several 'matches' were revealed but none leading to a positive paternity for my mother, so I continued to be disappointed.

But unbelievably, in 2019, "Eureka"! The name 'Gorton' popped up. This person was matched to me, according to "Ancestry. Com", as a 3rd – 4th cousin.

On tracing back, this person's grandfather was William Vernon Gorton's brother. So this person and I shared at the very least, a common great grand-father in Charles Frederick Gorton who came from Dorset, Dorchester, England.

I am not in a position to speculate on who in the Gorton family was my mother's father. Perhaps future DNA matching will solve the mystery.

---

[56] *Bellinga 2016 pp68-70*
[57] *"Autosomal DNA – ISOGG – Wiki SOGG - org*

Conclusion

After my mother's 'exemption', she gave up the name Gladys Marian Myquick, and reinvented herself as Gladys Sylvia Gordon. So somewhere along the line, she must have been told her father's name and mistakenly thought she heard 'Gordon' instead of 'Gorton'.

I am grateful to all those who came before me. Many suffered great hardships in their desire for betterment, uprooted from their homelands in this quest, some voluntarily, some forced, but all striving to make the best of their circumstances.

I am proud of my mix. It is this diversity of origin that is the lot of most Australians today.

My children, grandchildren and great grandchildren are all fiercely proud that within their veins runs the blood of the very first Australians mingled with that of the Europeans who left the countries of their birth to try to forge a better life for themselves here.

My mother never sought sympathy for the wrongs done to her and never expressed the need for an apology from anyone. Her philosophy was, "The past is the past". She only ever looked forward. But I do remember her wistfully telling us that as a child, Santa Claus never visited her. She said when she asked why he bought gifts to other kids but not her, she was told that Santa Claus only came to rich people. The 'other kids' to whom she referred, would most likely have been John Kenny's children at Hull River Settlement.

The only biological grandparent I knew was my father's mother. His father was killed in a timber-logging accident when he was just an infant.

So I was never to know my grandmother Tibby or my grandfather the 'Unknown' European.

They, in turn were denied knowledge of me and the multitudes of their other descendants from Gladys.

But the greatest shame of all is that they never enjoyed the privilege of knowing and loving their amazing daughter, Gladys.

I.
PUBLIC ACTS
OF THE
PARLIAMENT OF QUEENSLAND,
61° VICTORIAE.

ABORIGINALS.

An Act to make Provision for the better Protection and Care of the Aboriginal and Half-caste Inhabitants of the Colony, and to make more effectual Provision for Restricting the Sale and Distribution of Opium.

[ASSENTED TO 15TH DECEMBER, 1897.]

61 Vic. No. 17.
THE ABORIGINALS PROTECTION AND RESTRICTION OF THE SALE OF OPIUM ACT, 1897.

WHEREAS it is desirable to make provision for the better protection and care of the aboriginal and half-caste inhabitants of the Colony: And whereas great and widespread injury is being caused to the aboriginal and half-caste and certain other inhabitants of the Colony by the consumption of opium: And whereas the restrictions heretofore imposed by law upon the sale and distribution of opium are found to be insufficient, and it is expedient to make more effectual provision for restricting such sale and distribution, and for preventing the evils arising therefrom: Be it therefore enacted by the Queen's Most Excellent Majesty, by and with the advice and consent of the Legislative Council and Legislative Assembly of Queensland in Parliament assembled, and by the authority of the same as follows:— *Preamble.*

1. This Act shall be styled, and may be cited as, "*The Aboriginals Protection and Restriction of the Sale of Opium Act*, 1897," and shall commence and take effect on and from the first day of January, one thousand eight hundred and ninety-eight. *Short title and commencement.*

2. The Acts mentioned in the Schedule hereto are hereby repealed, to the extent mentioned in the third column of the said Schedule, except as to anything lawfully done thereunder before the commencement of this Act, and except so far as may be necessary for the purpose *Repeal.* *[Schedule.]*

Aboriginals Protection; Sale of Opium. 61 Vic. No. 17,

of supporting and continuing any proceeding taken, or of prosecuting or punishing any person for any offence committed before the commencement of this Act.

Interpretation.

3. The following terms shall, in this Act (unless the context otherwise indicates), bear the several meanings set against them respectively:—

"Reserve"—Any reserve heretofore or hereafter granted in trust, or reserved from sale or lease by the Governor in Council, for the benefit of the aboriginal inhabitants of the Colony, under the provisions of any law in force in Queensland relating to Crown lands;

"Minister"—The Home Secretary or other Minister of the Crown administering this Act;

"Protector"—A Protector of Aboriginals appointed under the provisions of this Act;

"Superintendent"—A Superintendent appointed under the provisions of this Act for any Reserve;

"District"—A District proclaimed under the provisions of this Act;

"Regulations"—Regulations made under this Act;

"Prescribed"—Prescribed by this Act or the Regulations under it;

"Liquor"—Liquor as defined by "*The Licensing Act of* 1885,"* and any Act amending the same;

"Opium"—Opium, whether in the form of gum or liquid, and every substance, whether solid or liquid, which contains opium, not being a substance compounded exclusively for medicinal purposes, and every substance which is or contains the ash of opium, or charcoal of opium;

"Half-caste"—Any person being the offspring of an aboriginal mother and other than an aboriginal father: Provided that the term "half-caste," wherever it occurs in this Act elsewhere than in the next following section, shall, unless the context otherwise requires, be construed to exclude every half-caste who, under the provisions of the said section, is deemed to be an aboriginal.

---

* 49 Vic. No. 18, *supra*, page 1252.

1897. *Aboriginals Protection; Sale of Opium.*

4. Every person who is—   *Persons deemed to be aboriginals.*
- (a) An aboriginal inhabitant of Queensland; or
- (b) A half-caste who, at the commencement of this Act, is living with an aboriginal as wife, husband, or child; or
- (c) A half-caste who, otherwise than as wife, husband, or child, habitually lives or associates with aboriginals;

shall be deemed to be an aboriginal within the meaning of this Act.

5. The Governor in Council may, by Proclamation, declare any portion or portions of the Colony to be a District, or Districts, for the purposes of this Act. *Proclamation of Districts.*

6. The Governor in Council may from time to time appoint, for the purpose of carrying the provisions of this Act into effect, fit and proper persons, to be severally called "Protector of Aboriginals," who shall, within the Districts respectively assigned to them, have and exercise the powers and duties prescribed. *Protectors to be appointed.*

7. The Governor in Council may appoint such and so many Superintendents for the reserves, situated within such Districts as aforesaid, as may be necessary for carrying the provisions of this Act into effect. *Superintendents to be appointed.*

8. Every reserve shall be subject to the provisions of this Act and the Regulations. *Reserves to be subject to Act and Regulations.*

9. It shall be lawful for the Minister to cause every aboriginal within any District, not being an aboriginal excepted from the provisions of this section, to be removed to, and kept within the limits of, any reserve situated within such District, in such manner, and subject to such conditions, as may be prescribed. The Minister may, subject to the said conditions, cause any aboriginal to be removed from one reserve to another. *Aboriginals may be removed to reserves.*

10. Every aboriginal who is— *Aboriginals excepted from liability to removal to a reserve.*
- (a) Lawfully employed by any person under the provisions of this Act or the Regulations, or under any other law in force in Queensland;
- (b) The holder of a permit to be absent from a reserve; or

(c) A female lawfully married to, and residing with, a husband who is not himself an aboriginal;

(d) Or for whom in the opinion of the Minister satisfactory provision is otherwise made;

shall be excepted from the provisions of the last preceding section.

Persons who are prohibited from entering a reserve. 11. It shall not be lawful for any person other than an aboriginal, not being a Superintendent or a person acting under his direction, and not being a person authorised under the Regulations, to enter or remain or be within the limits of a reserve upon which aboriginals are residing, for any purpose whatever.

Any person, without lawful excuse, entering or remaining or being upon such reserve as aforesaid, shall, for every such offence, be liable on conviction to a penalty not exceeding fifty pounds, or to imprisonment for any term not exceeding three months, and the proof of such lawful excuse shall be on the person charged.

Aboriginals and half-castes may be employed. 12. A Protector may permit any aboriginal or half-caste who, before the commencement of this Act, was employed by any trustworthy person, to continue to be so employed by such person, and, in like manner, may permit any aboriginal or half-caste not previously employed to be employed by a like person.

Duration, renewal, and revocation of permit. 13. Every permit, so granted as aforesaid, shall remain in force for twelve months only, but may at any time, before the expiration of such period, be renewed for any period not exceeding twelve calendar months, to commence from the expiration of the previous period of twelve months, and so, from time to time, so long as such aboriginal or half-caste is willing to continue to be employed by such person. Any such permission as aforesaid may be revoked at any time by a Protector by writing under his hand, and thereupon, if such related to an aboriginal, such aboriginal may be removed, by order of the Protector under and subject to the conditions prescribed, to a reserve, or, at the discretion of the Protector, the aboriginal or half-caste to whom such license related may be permitted, in like manner, to enter the employment of some other such trustworthy person as aforesaid. Such revocation shall not entitle any such employer to claim or recover any compensation for the loss of the service of such aboriginal or half-caste, or to maintain any action in respect of any alleged loss or damage that may be occasioned by such revocation.

1897.   *Aboriginals Protection; Sale of Opium.*

14. Any person who, except under the provisions of any Act or Regulations thereunder in force in Queensland, employs an aboriginal or a female half-caste, otherwise than in accordance with the provisions of this Act or the Regulations, or suffers or permits an aboriginal or a female half-caste to be in or upon any house or premises in his occupation or under his control, shall be guilty of an offence against this Act, and shall be liable, on conviction, to a penalty not exceeding fifty pounds and not less than ten pounds, or to imprisonment for any term not exceeding six months. *Harbouring of aboriginals and female half-castes prohibited.*

15. Every person desirous of employing an aboriginal or female half-caste under the provisions of this Act, shall forthwith, upon permission being granted by a Protector, enter into an agreement with such aboriginal or female half-caste, in the presence of any justice of the peace or member of the Police Force, for any period not exceeding twelve months. Every such agreement shall contain particulars of the names of the parties thereto, the nature of the service to be rendered by such aboriginal or female half-caste, the period during which such employment is to continue, the wages or other remuneration to be paid or given by the employer for such service, the nature of the accommodation to be provided for such aboriginal or female half-caste, and the conditions on which the agreement may be determined by either party. Every such agreement shall be in duplicate and be attested by such justice or member of the Police Force, who shall forthwith forward one of the said agreements to the nearest Protector. *Aboriginals and female half-castes to be employed under written agreement.*

16. Every aboriginal or female half-caste employed by any person, under the provisions of this Act, shall be under the supervision of a Protector, or such other person as may be authorised in that behalf by the Regulations; and every employer of such aboriginal or female half-caste shall permit any Protector, or such other person as aforesaid, to have access to such aboriginal or female half-caste at all reasonable times, for the purpose of making such inspection and inquiries as he may deem necessary. *Aboriginals and female half-castes in employment to be subject to supervision.*

17. Any person who, without the authority of a Protector, by writing under his hand, removes, or causes to be removed, an aboriginal or female half-caste from one District to another District, or to any place beyond the Colony, shall be guilty of an offence against this Act, and shall be liable, on conviction, to a penalty not exceeding one hundred pounds, or to imprisonment for any term not exceeding six months. *Prohibition of removal of aboriginals from one District to another or beyond the Colony.*

Aboriginals Protection; Sale of Opium. 61 Vic. No. 17,

Possession of blanket, &c., issued to an aboriginal or half-caste a punishable offence.

18. Every blanket issued by an officer of the Government to any aboriginal or half-caste shall be and remain the property of Her Majesty, and any person, other than an aboriginal or half-caste, who has in his possession or custody any such blanket or portion thereof which shall reasonably appear to the justices, from the marks thereupon or otherwise, to have been so issued for the use of an aboriginal or half-caste, shall be guilty of an offence against this Act, and shall be liable, on conviction, to a penalty not exceeding ten pounds.

Penalty for supplying liquor to aboriginals and half-castes.

19. Any person who supplies, or causes or permits to be supplied, any liquor to an aboriginal or a half-caste, except for *bonâ fide* medicinal purposes, proof of which shall be on the person accused, shall, for every such offence, be liable to a penalty not exceeding fifty pounds, or to imprisonment for any term not exceeding three months, and in every case to the costs of the conviction. In the case of a licensed victualler or wine-seller who is convicted of such offence, the penalty, by this section provided, shall be substituted for the penalty provided in respect of such offence by the sixty-seventh section of "*The Licensing Act of* 1885."*

Persons supplying opium to aboriginals or half-castes, guilty of a punishable offence, and penalty therefor.

20. Any person who supplies, or causes or permits to be supplied, any opium to an aboriginal or a half-caste, shall be guilty of an offence against this Act, and shall be liable, on conviction, for the first offence, to a penalty not exceeding one hundred pounds and not less than twenty pounds, one-half of which shall be paid to the person giving the information which leads to such conviction, or to imprisonment for any term not exceeding three months, and for the second and every subsequent offence to imprisonment for any term not exceeding six months, and in every case to the costs of the conviction.

Possession or sale of opium by certain persons unlawful.

21. Notwithstanding anything in "*The Sale and Use of Poisons Act*, 1891,"† to the contrary contained, it shall not be lawful for any person, not being a legally qualified medical practitioner, or a pharmaceutical chemist, or a wholesale dealer in drugs, to sell, or in any manner dispose of, deliver, or supply, opium to any other person, or to have or keep in his possession any opium for any purpose whatever; and it shall not be lawful for any legally qualified medical practitioner or pharmaceutical chemist, residing or carrying on business at a greater

---

* 49 Vic. No. 18, *supra*, page 1252.   † 55 Vic. No. 31, *supra*, page 4339.

1897.   *Aboriginals Protection ; Sale of Opium.*

distance, by the nearest practicable road, than one hundred miles from Brisbane, Rockhampton, or Townsville, to have or keep in or upon any premises in his occupation or under his control, at any one time, any greater quantity of opium than two pounds weight avoirdupois:

Provided that it shall not be unlawful for a common carrier to have in his possession opium, for the purpose of conveying the same, for delivery to the person to whom it has been lawfully consigned.

22. Any person who unlawfully has in his possession any opium, or unlawfully sells, or in any manner disposes of, delivers, or supplies opium to any person other than an aboriginal or a half-caste, shall, for every such offence, be liable, on conviction, to a penalty not exceeding fifty pounds, one-half of which shall be paid to the person giving the information which leads to such conviction. Any legally qualified medical practitioner or pharmaceutical chemist, residing or carrying on business at a greater distance, by the nearest practicable road, than one hundred miles from Brisbane, Rockhampton, or Townsville as aforesaid, who has or keeps, in or upon any premises in his occupation or under his control, any greater quantity of opium than two pounds weight avoirdupois, shall be liable, on conviction, for the first offence, to a penalty not exceeding fifty pounds and not less than ten pounds, and for the second, and every subsequent, offence to imprisonment for any term not exceeding six months. *Penalty for unlawful possession or sale or delivery of opium.*

23. Upon complaint made or laid on oath, before any justice of the peace, by any person, that he believes that opium is kept or concealed in any house, building, or place, contrary to any of the provisions of this Act, whether by a person authorised under the provisions of " *The Sale and Use of Poisons Act,* 1891,"* to sell or deal in poisons or not, such justice may grant a warrant, to any member of the Police Force, to enter and search such house, building, or place, between the hours of six in the morning and twelve at night, and, if admission is refused, to break into the same, and to seize and detain all opium found therein contrary to the provisions of this Act. *Premises may be searched for opium believed to be kept contrary to provisions of Act.*

24. Any member of the Police Force, and any person acting under the direction and in the presence of a justice of the peace, may detain any person, found travelling, whom such member of the Police Force or such justice of *Travellers suspected to be in unlawful possession of opium may be searched, &c.*

---
* 55 Vic. No. 31, *supra*, page 4339.

the peace may suspect to have in his possession any opium contrary to the provisions of this Act, and may search such person, and may open and search any pack, swag, or other receptacle carried or conveyed by such person, and may seize any such opium as aforesaid found in the possession of such person, and may forthwith arrest such person without warrant, and detain him in custody until he can be brought before justices to be dealt with according to law.

Opium found in unlawful possession to be forfeited. 25. If, upon the hearing of a complaint against any person in whose possession opium has been found in contravention of any of the provisions of this Act, the justices, before whom such complaint is heard, convict such person of the offence stated in such complaint, they shall, in addition to any penalty imposed upon the offender, order that all the opium so found in his possession be forfeited to the Crown, and the same shall be forfeited accordingly.

Averment in complaint sufficient evidence of certain matters. 26. In every prosecution for an offence against any of the provisions of this Act relating to an aboriginal or a half-caste, the averment in the complaint, that any person named therein is an aboriginal or a half-caste, shall be sufficient evidence of the fact unless the contrary is proved.

Persons by whom certain proceedings may be instituted. 27. All actions and proceedings against any person for the recovery of any wages due to an aboriginal or a half-caste, who is, or has been, employed by such person under the provisions of this Act, or for any breach of an agreement entered into by such person under the provisions of this Act, may be instituted and carried on by, or in the name of, a Protector, or by, or in the name of, any other person authorised by the Minister by writing under his hand.

Persons by whom certain complaints may be made. 28. Every complaint for an offence against the provisions of this Act or the Regulations, other than the provisions contained in the twenty-second, twenty-third, twenty-fourth, and twenty-fifth sections hereof, may be made or laid by a Protector or Superintendent, or by a member of the Police Force, and the prosecution may be conducted by the person by whom the complaint is so made or laid. Every complaint for an offence against any of the provisions of this Act, contained in the sections hereinbefore in this section mentioned, shall be made or laid by a member of the Police Force or a justice of the peace only.

29. Any person who shall be convicted of an offence against this Act or the Regulations, shall, unless hereinbefore or in the Regulations otherwise provided, be liable to a penalty not exceeding ten pounds. *Provision for penalties where not specified.*

30. All offences against this Act, or the Regulations, not herein otherwise specially provided for, may be prosecuted in a summary way before any two justices. *Offences to be prosecuted before any two justices.*

31. The Governor in Council may from time to time, by Proclamation, make Regulations for all or any of the matters following, that is to say,— *Regulations.*

(1) Prescribing the mode of removing aboriginals to a reserve, and from one reserve to another;

(2) Defining the duties of Protectors and Superintendents, and any other persons employed to carry the provisions of this Act into effect;

(3) Authorising entry upon a reserve by specified persons or classes of persons for specified objects, and defining those objects, and the conditions under which such persons may visit or remain upon a reserve, and fixing the duration of their stay thereupon, and providing for the revocation of such authority in any case;

(4) Prescribing the mode of distribution and expenditure of moneys granted by Parliament for the benefit of aboriginals;

(5) Apportioning amongst, or for the benefit of, aboriginals or half-castes, living on a reserve, the net produce of the labour of such aboriginals or half-castes;

(6) Providing for the care, custody, and education of the children of aboriginals;

(7) Providing for the transfer of any half-caste child, being an orphan, or deserted by its parents, to an orphanage;

(8) Prescribing the conditions on which any aboriginal or half-caste children may be apprenticed to, or placed in service with, suitable persons;

(9) Providing for the mode of supplying to any half-castes, who may be declared to be entitled thereto, any rations, blankets, or other necessaries, or any medical or other relief or assistance;

Aboriginals Protection ; Sale of Opium. 61 Vic. No. 17, 1897.

(10) Prescribing the conditions on which the Minister may authorise any half-caste to reside upon any reserve, and limiting the period of such residence, and the mode of dismissing or removing any such half-caste from such reserve ;

(11) Providing for the control of all aboriginals and half-castes residing upon a reserve, and for the inspection of all aboriginals and half-castes, employed under the provisions of this Act or the Regulations ;

(12) Maintaining discipline and good order upon a reserve ;

(13) Imposing the punishment of imprisonment, for any term not exceeding three months, upon any aboriginal or half-caste who is guilty of a breach of the Regulations relating to the maintenance of discipline and good order upon a reserve ;

(14) Imposing, and authorising a Protector to inflict summary punishment by way of imprisonment, not exceeding fourteen days, upon aboriginals or half-castes, living upon a reserve or within the District under his charge, who, in the judgment of the Protector, are guilty of any crime, serious misconduct, neglect of duty, gross insubordination, or wilful breach of the Regulations;

(15) Prohibiting any aboriginal rites or customs that, in the opinion of the Minister, are injurious to the welfare of aboriginals living upon a reserve;

(16) Providing for the due carrying out of the provisions of this Act;

(17) Providing for all other matters and things that may be necessary to give effect to this Act.

Regulations to have the force of law. 32. Such Regulations, not being contrary to the provisions of this Act, shall have the force of law.

Certain half-castes may be exempted from provisions of Act. 33. It shall be lawful for the Minister to issue to any half-caste, who, in his opinion, ought not to be subject to the provisions of this Act, a certificate, in writing under his hand, that such half-caste is exempt from the provisions of this Act and the Regulations, and from and after the issue of such certificate, such half-caste shall be so exempt accordingly.

61 Vic. No. 8, 1897.   *Government Savings Bank Stock Act.*

THE SCHEDULE. [*See* s. 2.]

Date of Act.	Title of Act.	Extent of Repeal.
55 Vic. No. 31	"*An Act for Regulating the Sale and Use of Poisons*"	Section 13.
59 Vic. No. 29	"*An Act to Amend the Laws relating to the Sale of Intoxicating Liquor*"	So much of Section 13 as is contained in the words, " aboriginal native of Australia or half-caste of that race, or to any"; and in the further words, " of Australia or."

www.ingramcontent.com/pod-product-compliance
Lightning Source LLC
Chambersburg PA
CBHW080856010526
44107CB00057B/2589